From Bondage To Freedom

My Mission. My Journey.

MARY BARBER

Copyright © 2019 Mary Barber

All rights reserved.

ISBN: 9781690913498

I have tried to recreate events, locales and conversations from my memories of them. In order to maintain their anonymity, in some instances I have changed the names of individuals and places. I may have changed some identifying characteristics and details such as physical properties, occupations and places of residence to protect the privacy of individuals.

All photographs have been used with permission.

DEDICATION

I dedicate this biography to my children, Dairus E. Thompson II and Dainiqua T. Barber and Nanna's 5 grand babies. I just want to honor the journey that we have lived together, being the best mother I could be, despite our times of bondage and storms of life – we made it! We shall conquer this as a family as long as God gives me the ability to continue his journey, for a greater future.
Love, Moms.

CONTENTS

Acknowledgments	i
Introduction	1
Overcoming Addictions	5
Overcoming Difficult Times	21
Overcoming Life Challenges	39
Overcoming Frustration	47
Overcoming Gossiping	55
Overcoming Grief	61
Overcoming Divorce Through Adversity	69
Overcoming Procrastination	81
Overcoming Low Self-Esteem & Identity Issues	87
I Conquered It All Through Christ	95

ACKNOWLEDGMENTS

I want to thank some of the many people who have been a part of my journey; my dad Leroy Barber Sr., my mom Vollie Mary Barber (Dula), my kids Dainiqua T. Barber and Dairus E. Thompson II, Aunt Edith Smith, Mable Taylor (Cuz), Sallie Mae Hamilton (Cuz), Marcia Green (Jackson – Cuz), Danita (Cuz), Norman Grinstead & Family (Cuz), Pogo (Cuz), Annette Hunt (Netty – BFF), Leonard Howard (BFF), Michelle Williams, Wonda Williams, Stacey C. and Mikey R. and all my many brothers and sisters (siblings), both alive and passed on – and all my nephews and nieces and a host of special cousins!

INTRODUCTION

I write this book in honor of the ancestors that started this whole life for me.

I dedicate this book to society, and to my ancestors who experienced the life of great adventurers; real struggles and being enslaved. Not only did our ancestors live as slaves, but we as people in today's world are still living in bondage and incarcerated in our mindset. But I decree, and come to let a world know - no more chains, they're broken; shackles are released and I prophesize we have been set free from BONDAGE to FREEDOM.

In 1905, my grandfather, Daddy Roy, was born and lived in Vicksburg Mississippi which was my dad, Leroy Barber's, father. My grandmother, who was my dad's mother, Earnestine; wasn't a Barber but became a Barber eventually, and she was born in 1910. At the age of 11, my father (which he's still living and is 87 years of age) was brought to Michigan after living in Vicksburg, Mississippi. God is amazing! My grandfather left the south in 1944 and went to the city of Delray, Michigan to find work in the plants, where some of my family still resides on my dad's side. My dad and his mom, which was my grandmother, were left there in Mississippi until they journeyed to Michigan. My dad also experienced his aunts and uncles and others on the plantation picking cotton for a living at 3 cents an hour for the short time that he as a young boy was living in the city of Vicksburg, and we complain! Some picked cotton on the plantation for 5 cents an hour as well.

Daddy Roy & Earnestine

My great grandmother, whom I was named after; Vollie Mary Jordan, who was my mother's grandmother, came from Atlanta, Georgia. She also experienced the plantation life of picking cotton and slavery. She was born on June 21, 1888, and God whispered in her ear and called such an angel, family, heritage, and faithful woman of God home in the year of 1996. My grandmother, Sallie B. Hutchinson, which was my mother's mother; she was born on August 29, 1910, and God also whispered in her ear and said 'Angel, your work is done; here's your wings' in 1982, the year I graduated from high school.

Great Granny Vollie Mary Jordan

My dad was an employee working for Great Lakes Steel for 35 years as a millwright and a Forman; the only African American that wore a white hat as a Forman in the plant, and now it's called National Steel in Ecorse Michigan on Jefferson today. We are a blessed family of 13, including stepchildren - we never missed a meal and after my dad retired, my mom worked for Our Lady Of Lords as an accountant for 10 years on Jefferson and Schaefer to help her husband and kids after his retirement; and also worked for River Rouge adult education night school to see others in the city achieve and receive what God assigned her to do as a disciple.

I tribute to all of my ancestors who served faithfully; not only with the blessed family they encountered but the seeds that have been sown over the years that are harvesting. Thanking my savior for giving me the years of bonding and spending time by hanging with my parents as a little girl and being so close to my parents and grandparents. And being at my grandmother Sallie B house every Saturday helping my mother clean, and take care of her mom, and how they would pray; not knowing they were preparing me and showing me the mandate that I had to carry after they were gone. With these matriarchs, I know they received their crown and are still in heaven praying and shouting me on, and I know my savior said: "GOOD and FAITHFUL servants, well done!"

Thanks for passing the baton to me as the matriarch. It ain't easy, but you always told me "Nothing's too hard for God".

Honoring my lineage; my father Leroy Barber Sr., my grandmother Sallie B. Hutchinson, and my dear mother Vollie Mary Barber

MARY BARBER

1 OVERCOMING ADDICTIONS

When I was growing up as a young lady in a neighborhood called River Rouge, I started Walter White Elementary School. That was my kindergarten year, and back then we graduated in the seventh grade. My best friends were Netty and Stacey; we always got in trouble, but living on the same street with Netty brought so much love and friendship and was family-oriented. Her grandmother, who we called momma Vick, wasn't no joke and her mom Evonne who I shared the same birthday with (who's deceased now) but was hustling strong-headed women and didn't take no mess from no-one. So, you couldn't blame who we were because we followed our people's tracks. We were grounded from good seed even though people did what they wanted, we still had good seeds planted from where we came from. Netty, Stacey and I went from kindergarten to twelfth grade together. I can recall when me and Netty would walk to school and home every day. We also had friends by the name of Faye and Maryann who was bullies and we were all just knuckleheads and talking about fighting - we had a fight every day. It didn't make sense because we would fight in school and get a crack from every teacher, then we would fight on the way from school and then in the neighborhood, we were just some hard-headed warriors in elementary school!

Can you imagine how life repeats itself, and my grandsons attended the same elementary school, and both playing Quarterback, where they still sponsor Head Start? WOW!!! Something, huh! I was a bright girl in elementary school even though I still had a hard head and worried my parents as we all did. I was still intelligent and had a promise and covenant around me. I won the spelling bee; in the sixth grade, I came in third place and in the seventh grade I came in second place. Pretty close, huh! Was always a WINNER!!! I attended River Rouge High School; high school started early back in our days. Times have really changed now, where high school starts at tenth grade now, or middle school starts at seventh through ninth grade which is excellent. The students can focus more on their studies because the younger generation is not surrounded by so many adults in high school, where there's so much peer pressure like what I experienced growing up. They can stay more focused and not experience so much peer pressure, which of course we know exists - but it's a chance for the students to still not be around so many grown folks. Even when I was growing up, the neighborhood was infested with drugs and even in the households on an everyday basis; and it's still true now.

Well, well, well, I first got high off marijuana in the eighth grade at the age of 14. WOW!!! Yeah, Ms. HOLIER THAN THOU Liz!!! How can we have a testimony, or minister, or save our children today if we never experienced life challenges that every individual has experienced?

HOPEFULLY!!!

I smoked marijuana for over 10 years; not only did I smoke it, but I also sold it. I made a living selling 2lbs a week, had the whole neighborhood sold up. I had the best tie stick, monkey paw, skunk – which was the best high in the whole world until I met Christ and received the Holy Spirit which is a high that will never come down. The only difference with that generation compared to now is we didn't kill or fight over drugs and who had the most money. Huh!!! We ALL had it, we all had enough money to go around the country. We enjoyed life. Not saying it was right, but there were no worries. We all got HIGH and if my friends or whoever needed, I supplied it. I just have to take a moment to give a shout out to my Lord who kept me in my foolishness when I was walking in my own will and not the will of God. I made it through every storm, every trial, every tribulation because I had a praying mother. I used to smoke marijuana in the morning before school which was at 7am, and again at noon, and after school. Go home, do my chores, pack up my sack and go to the Beechwood Center where everybody in the hood would hang out, watch all the fine men in the neighborhood play basketball. And there was nothing like being a teenager enjoying your boo playing basketball in the hood!

I worked for the summer program league where there were jobs around for all the kids, and we had our own money and there were opportunities in the city where we could enjoy life, live and have fun. Loving families that stuck together and it was a different generation back then. We didn't have to go to bed with guns all around the bed and in the house in every corner like we do now. But; I smoked, and I got paid. I used to be so HIGH but I always kept focus, always treated people right and shared what I had. It's crazy how people will kill you over a blunt of "KUSH" when it deteriorates your brain, it makes you drop out of school and you want to kill your best friend or your family member because you're high as a kite. Don't get me wrong – yes, it's ok to smoke if that's what you like, and like everyone says it comes from the earth. And I always say that GOD made the earth and all on it, but he didn't say lace it with meth/opioids and kill and commit homicide because of money and drugs. If you folks can see how society is being destroyed from drug abuse, causing poverty amongst families, and you cannot even get a job with smoke in your system. WHY abuse the purpose and the mentality that GOD has given you? Wake up, folks! Get a life. YEAH, I did it – but I survived it. Everybody doesn't survive the dope game or addiction, so STOP!!! Pray for deliverance, walk into your purpose of what God has predestined from the foundation when you were in your mother's womb.

JEREMIAH 29:11 For I know the thoughts that I think toward you, saith the LORD, thoughts of peace, and not of evil, to give you an expected end.

Now, how do you expect to have peace when you're high all the time? I had to wonder myself, sometimes, when I was abusing drugs. When you're high, and the high go down, the only peace you can have is to get high again. Then how can your brain function correctly if you are not focused and addicted to drugs? The drugs are controlling you. We don't want to be controlled by drugs, people. We want to be controlled by the Holy Spirit because it guards your mind and your heart, it gives you peace that surpasses all understanding; it leads, directs and guides you... How in the world can we as people have a communication level and a peaceful relationship when we don't have the consciousness to think right? I am a Surgical Tech now, and I specialized in Neurology Surgery and that's your central nervous system and if that system is not functioning right, then nothing's going to function right. The saying is that a mind is a terrible thing to waste.

I remember my smart know-it-all butt told a few friends I was bringing the tie stick to school and at River Rouge High we would sneak onto the fourth floor to smoke, or perform other ritual things. I'm quite sure the ones I grew up with remember the fourth floor in River Rouge High... lol. This particular day, you know we had our weed pipe too. I specialized in the ceramic pipe; you can keep them in your pocket. Now I know y'all remember those ones with the different designs and colors. I used to own at least 10 or more. MAN... I lit up the marijuana in the pipe it was so strong and we were so high. Now imagine this was tie stick, I got it from my Caucasian (white) friends, the best in the nation. The principal comes on the floor and almost caught us; the whole school was smelling like weed. Do you know, and of course, most people reading this book know my dad...thank God I took off like I was in the Olympics and I escaped because I would have been dead if my parents found out. People, now it's so ironic how we can get saved in the Church and become a kingdom citizen, go to worship every Sunday and cannot share the secrets and skeletons that we have suffered with over the years with somebody that is out here dealing with addictions. Don't get me wrong, we don't have to tell everything but I'm here to tell a nation I bow naked before Christ surrendering my all to you LORD withholding nothing because I'm after souls and I refuse for another generation or my grandchildren to experience what I experienced in life. The devil is a liar. We shall not live and not die. These drugs out here; there's too much-mixed mess in it. You can take Zantac or pop pills; drink lean which is a very dangerous addiction and you might not make it through the next hour. I had a friend in high school I'll never forget her – she's deceased now. She was one of my homies and she distributed pills and they would pop mescaline, Christmas Trees, etc. And they would laugh all day. Well, thank God I wasn't a pill popper and popped Christmas trees (I was already silly as ever) and I probably would have been dead. That was one thing I was scared of – pills. I'm scared to take an aspirin now, my daughter laughs at me when I take a Tylenol #4. I'd be scared that I wouldn't wake up. Narcotics are scary to me.

But you know it goes on and on because I was a very aggressive female, had what I wanted, and could get what I wanted because I was so beautiful. But see - we as beautiful women, the enemy wants your mind and your body. GOD wants everything. So, whatever; I wanted that voice and manipulating spirit where any man that had money or the drug, I had his mind because that's how the devil works, he uses you to get what he wants and he will use women to destroy men or men to destroy women. Destroying our own friends and generations to get whatever we wanted. So, of course, you know the love of money is the root of all evil. And I loved money, so I decided to get really deep into the game. I decided to get paid $2000 a week testing cocaine off the rock, of course, coming straight out of Colombia. I had the best, I wasn't a fool, If I did die, I was going out right! Oh! Oh! Oh! Yeah, the prayer warrior – she experienced real life! How can you expect to be called out of the darkness into the marvelous light if you've never been through the darkest places in life?

> *1 PETER 2:9 But ye are a chosen generation, a royal priesthood, an holy nation, a peculiar people; that ye should shew forth the praises of him who hath called you out of darkness into his marvellous light:*

Thank God that he kept me!!! Now, how in the world can people say 'you crazy for worshipping like that' and that 'it don't take all of that', but let me tell you - I could've been in my grave if it wasn't for God's grace and mercy. So, don't worry about how I worship, when you never carried my burdens or the yolk and shackles and chains, God, using me to destroy. So, people want to make the same mistakes and choices I made. How can we be so quick to judge others? Or enjoy my successes when you weren't there in the darkest times of my life when I was sinking?

I will worship the Lord at all times and his praises shall continue to be in my mouth. God was there when I was around those shipping 10 to 100 kilos of cocaine every week. Transporting back and forth out of state. Didn't touch nothing because I was a real one, but I stayed strapped, made sure it happened and you tell me it was a man or my man that got me through? THE DEVIL IS A LIAR, IT WAS GOD'S GRACE!!! I could've been that female doing life in the penitentiary or 10 years of conspiracy. That's why there's nothing I wouldn't do for God because he kept me.

CORINTHIANS 6:19-20 "Or do you not know that your body is a temple of the Holy Spirit within you, whom you have from God? You are not your own, for you were bought with a price. So, glorify GOD in the body." ESV

So, if we are bought with a price, how in the double hockey sticks can we allow the enemy to buy our minds and our bodies and abuse us and use us for his goods, then throw us out? God says he will never leave or forsake us, so who are you going to serve today? Starting today, the ones that are dealing with strongholds and addictions, I come to tell you that the chains and shackles that have been holding up your purpose can be broken right now. I come against any drug addictions, distributors, whoremongers, lusting spirits, sexual immorality, witchcraft, traps, incantations, egoism, etc. Any generational curses that the enemy has kept us in bondage; that demon has to go right now IN THE MIGHTY NAME OF JESUS!!!

Life is full of challenges, temptations, oppositions, trials, and tribulations. So, I come to let my people know that no matter what you go through in life – God is a healer, deliverer, and a liberator. We are free from barricades, chains and bondage. Even being disobedient and trying and testing life adventures, God still had me and he will hold you in his bosom and in the cleft of the rock. Yeah!!! The enemy bragged and encouraged and supported my wrongdoing because I was one of the suppliers. I fed everyone, and clothed and housed everyone, so as long as I had the money and the things their heart desires, the enemy loved me, but boy oh boy when the source went down! Where are my friends now? But baby, let me tell you I have a friend that's a friend to the friendless. One that will never leave or forsake you and he never lies and his word will not come back to you void. You know life was fabulous once, but losing so many friends to the penitentiary and dying and still out here trying to find their way.... People; there's no way out, but through Christ - "GOD IS THE ONLY WAY.". It was a life experience, but they say never regret what you have been through – which I never did. But I can say God took me through a season where I had to go back into the enemy's camps and minister to my friends and family, which they could still not understand to this day why I was separated from them. The word says come from amongst those and be ye separated. God has set you apart, and shaped and molded you for His purpose, and prepared you for the fight. So, when I went back into the devil's camp, I had to be ready – armed and equipped to fight against the wiles and the tactics of the enemies where those same spirits could not take over me. To this day, if you are not born again and walking with God you would never understand my testimony and it's not for you to understand, it's for God to get the GLORY!!! Even though; when I was allowed to go back into the devil's camp, I was delivered from marijuana and cocaine so I would go back into the territory to let my friends know that if God can deliver me, he can deliver you because he is not a respecter God.

    I still wasn't quite delivered from my red wine, and drinks, but I was at a stage of my life where I wasn't where I used to be with the drugs and fornication. GOD will create in you a new spirit and a clean heart and it's not an overnight change; it's an everyday process that God is working on me. When God snatches you out of the enemy's hand and you are not prepared to go back, you will end up right back in the same situation. Then it repeats itself over and over and over again until you get knocked upside the head and say: "Well, God. I learned this time and I don't want to take that route".

    God wants his will to be done, not our will. People, you wouldn't understand others' personal relationship with God, you would only understand your relationship and then that's when your tests become a testimony. It was not that I was anti-social or so Holy! Holy! I just was being obedient to the task of what God had designed for me to do to establish the things that were already in my plan of life. My ministry is to go back into a dying world and take back what the enemy has stolen, take back what the locust, palmer worms and caterpillars have eaten up and get my people to receive salvation and get saved. Why did Jesus come back?

> *MATTHEW 9:11-13 "When the Pharisees saw this, they asked his disciples, "Why does your teacher eat with tax collectors and sinners?" But Jesus said, "It is not the healthy who need a doctor, but it's the sick, I desire mercy on my people, not sacrifice. For I have not come to call the righteous, but the sinners." "*
>
> *ESV*

We were born in sin and shaped in iniquity, that's why we have to be born again; we become new creatures in Christ. Old things become old, and new things become new (remember, I am not perfect) but I'm walking in perfection each and every day to be like Christ and there's nothing like it. Just as the son of the old man did not come to be served, but to serve, and to give his life a ransom for many. We are to be servants of God and not to be selfish and serve ourselves. I am a new creature. I slipped up in life and let God down and fell short of the glory of God, but I had a praying mother and God snatched me out of the pit of the enemy. The good thing is, every time my finances get low and I am going through the storms, that same demon arises again and whispers in my ear and says "What about all the millions you counted in your life, what about the luxuries, the houses, the Gucci, Prada and all the things you used to have?" But, let me tell you what...

PSALMS 20:7 Some trust in chariots, and some in horses: but we will remember the name of the LORD our God.

We hustle, we get fast things and money in life and nothing lasts, I wasn't happy – only when the money was coming. The joy I have right now, the world didn't give it to me and the world cannot take it away. My life is more important and I'd rather have my life and peace of mind besides getting robbed or shot in the head and six feet under. People still hate you if you are doing the right thing or if you are doing wrong. What matters to people if they are not happy within themselves; they don't even like themselves. I changed my lifestyle, set goals and higher standards to accomplish my purpose of what God has predestined from the foundation. I went to school and earned a very high-demand degree. Baby, let me tell you; it's paying off. I want to tell you there's going to be bumps in the road. I deal with prejudice, discrimination, and intimidation every day, and it's so ironic and amazing to see how you set your standards high in life and people get worse and hate and want to compete with you. But one thing I can say is that I never judge people.

I was always aggressive and wanted the best for my family, children and others – but when God calls people to divine purpose, folk look at you differently and always think that you feel you are better than them, but let me tell you something – if you are walking with God you are special, a Royal priesthood, a holy nation, a peculiar person. So how can you be made in God's image and likeness and that's what we want for others? I was a hustler for the devil, and now I'm a gangsta WARRIOR for Christ, so don't hate the game, hate who made me and transformed me into a new creature.

> *1 JOHN 4:20 If a man say, I love God, and hateth his brother, he is a liar: for he that loveth not his brother whom he hath seen, how can he love God whom he hath not seen?*

Yeah! I snorted cocaine, but I had the best beige, and pure substance out of Colombia. I wasn't one of those tricks that snorted or got high off of whatever came my way. I was in control, and I had a God that had all the control when I wasn't in my right mind, thinking I was all that. Drove the best cars at 15 years old with a green LTD Chevy, in the ninth grade with a four-door Fury with the police light on it clean as a whistle, had a four-door Maxima (cocaine white) in the eleventh grade and a BMW; and a two-seat Corvette. I had a Fiat in the ninth grade and a Saab. I never had to walk to school or nowhere in my life, but I knew God because my mother raised us up to know God. But - I wasn't transfigured into the new creature. I was in my own will, but now I can speak to the next person that's continuing to go up the same mountain over and over. People, we keep asking God to change the mountain, but the mountain is changing you. Yes!!! I had the best vehicles and all the money, but I didn't have the Holy Spirit. God changed me, yes, it was very painful giving up everything. I had to walk in the newness of God because we live a life thinking we are invincible, but let me tell you something – nothing is like when God consecrated you, and purged you, and plucked everything that's not like him out of your life... It's a wonderful thing. My heart is new, my spirit is new and I walk in newness. I look like his glory and I will become everything that God promises me to be because I'm not trusting the dope man, I'm not trusting the job. I'm not depending on my friends, who become your enemies anyhow.

I LEARNED TO TRUST IN JESUS AND I LEARNED TO TRUST IN GOD!!!

Rejoice in the fact that God was not trying to destroy me, he was delivering me from all the mess that was around me and shaping and molding me into my purpose of who he predestined me to be.

> *JEREMIAH 29:11 For I know the thoughts that I think toward you, saith the LORD, thoughts of peace, and not of evil, to give you an expected end.*

People this is not the time to throw in the towel, this is not the time to question your faith, stay in the race! Wait on the Lord!!! Sometimes you win, sometimes we lose. It's all a part of God's plan. It's so amazing when I can look back over my life and think about how the enemy tried to tear me down, and that was only through the bad company and the choices you make in life, but trust me, I had fun. I don't regret anything I ever experienced in my life because it strengthened me, it made me become that great mother, auntie, sister, evangelist, disciple, ambassador for Christ. It's all a makeover!!! I had all the luxury, from BMWs to Volvos to every old-school car a rich man could own, but as they say, my people a reminder – if you don't have God, it's all useless. The most important luxury I have now is PEACE that surpasses all understanding. When the car dealers turn me down from working hard and doing right by God, I can still stand on God's word and still trust him and say for God I live and for God, I die, and he will make a way. I don't run to the drug or my family or friends thinking they can fix it because only God can fix it. When I got laid off work or fired from discrimination and harassment, envy, I didn't run to the drugs. I stood on the word of God and he supplied all my needs according to his riches and glory.

> *1 CORINTHIANS 15:33 Be not deceived: evil communications corrupt good manners.*

People, this is in the word of GOD and I will never forget my mom saying everything is going down but the word of GOD. Trust me, the dope game went down, and when you run out of resources you run out of friends. Friends walk out because there wasn't any more laying up in the plush home with white carpet all through the house; anything they wanted was available. Family and friends betray you because you didn't have the money to give but she still interceded on the behalf of my enemies, and that was a powerful season and it's still in effect. When God has you forgive your enemies, and equip you to go back in the world, bring them to Christ and then you dream about them and have to pray for them and see them being delivered. Tell me my God is POWERFUL!!! So, through my years of consecration and being sold out for God, and him preparing me to write this book and using me as his willing vessel and for his goodness. Well, I come today to tell a world that is still struggling with addictions if God did it for me, he can do it for anyone. I intercede for a corporate nation because GOD loves us in spite of our addictions, GOD loves us in spite of our disobedience and doing it our own way. So, I come to tell you that if you are facing addiction in your life... if it's sex, drugs, money, cars; anything that you want to make a change, every giant and demonic attack in life is going to face you. God will give you Power and Authority to fight against those adversaries and attacks; that's that part of becoming victorious.

It's so amazing as I'm even writing and meditating with tears in my eyes knowing that God is not a respecter God and if he can deliver me from the devourer of the enemy - and I was deep in the game - I know he can do for you. So, just remember when God rescues you from the mouth of the enemy and transforms your way of living, don't judge others, pray for your enemies and those that despise you. God will favor you. My enemies tried, but couldn't triumph over me. My enemies whispered, gossiped about me, conspired, lied, but God still favored me. My character, my integrity would not fail because there is no failure in God. I speak Health, Freedom, Life, Prosperity over our life. Everything was in question and I promised God I wouldn't compromise; I would only worship the ground he walked on.

> *PROVERBS 20:1 Wine is a mocker, strong drink is raging: and whosoever is deceived thereby is not wise.*

Teenagers, family, friends – it is not wise to use drugs or be addicted to anything if it's not being addicted to the word of God. You are one way or a minute from being exploited. I lost a brother from crack cocaine, I lost a brother as an alcoholic, I lost a brother from lung cancer and it goes on and on and on and on and on. So, don't judge me and talk about 'why do I take all of that' and 'why do I pray' because my family that's still alive shall live and not die, especially from the set-up of the enemy.

The GENERATIONAL CURSE stops today with me.

I arise from all of my problems, knowing God is able to strengthen me. We have to learn how to fight back, not physically but with the armor that God has equipped us with to stand against the wiles of the enemy and the tactics of our adversaries that we come up against every day. Stop medicating our pain on drugs, alcohol, pornography and let God heal and restore the voids and pain that we wrestle with every day.

> *EPHESIANS 6:12 For we wrestle not against flesh and blood, but against principalities, against powers, against the rulers of the darkness of this world, against spiritual wickedness in high places.*

I had friends that have served 10, 17, 18, 20, 30 years. Being incarcerated for being disobedient; and the ones that aren't incarcerated are still using it, dead, or caught up in the court system. I remember my pastor preaching a sermon on dry bones out of Ezekiel; where people are walking around every day and have dry bones and cannot find their way. But I come to tell you that those bones have to come alive! I speak life into the dry bones of people who are reading this novel that your life will be changed today in the mighty name of Jesus. I believe that you will get your consciousness and sanity back and live a prosperous life in the land of the living. I'm not judging, I'm just a vessel that God is using in this earthly realm. So, if there's a problem – take it up with the master. I have been through some of the toughest, roughest storms in my life and I'm quite sure we all have. I am a chosen one, a royal priesthood, peculiar woman of God, and he has delivered me out of the darkness into the marvelous light.

I am a new creature. My addictions were not the will of God. It was a testimony to someone's sister, brother or family member who might be dealing with some kind of afflictions and have tried everything and don't know who to turn to. God can deliver you from the devourer. God used me as that angel of the family to go into a dying world to save the oppressed, give the blind sight to see, and feed the hungry. Someone has to take the initiative, and my mother passed the baton to me to be the matriarch. I didn't want it; but it's not my will, it was God's will to do what he asks us to do to make a change for the next generation. I wouldn't tell you people it's not hard coming from a million-dollar industry in the game and letting go of everything to serve God, but I shall eat the good of the land without being faulty and doing my own will.

    Being a woman of God, pressing towards your purpose and goals every day trying your best to do what's right and the enemy comes to hunt you in every way he can. But I had to acknowledge that if God is for me, who can be against me? Greater is he that is in me than he that's in the world. I feel renewed, I look renewed. Now, I can witness the truth for someone else to be converted. That's why, when you see me come into the house of the Lord on Sundays it's not to represent what I'm wearing, or to get a man, or to showboat and pretend; it's to show God's glory and know I'm coming because I have a demon to fight. To show that dope dealer, the armed robbery man who did 18 years and was a Muslim can come to God and be converted Christian because you see my walk. The whoremonger and the young girl who was homeless and I took you in as a mother, showed you love and now you are making bucks. Because God showed you, even though your biological mother didn't want you, he gave you me because he is a mother to the motherless. Young teenagers out here clubbing every week and smoking dope and drinking lean can come up to me and say, mom, auntie, sis, what's up – can a sinner go to church? And I can pick them up when my gas was low and take them in my arms and say that God still saves, that God still loves you. I can walk into the dope house and they would hide the drugs and say "Come here, Miss Holy", which is okay with me because I'm here to please God and it's all about respect and the transformation of seeing my family and friends being converted and receive salvation right now. So, don't let church (four walls) keep you people from coming into the house of the Lord because of betrayal and voices talking about that we cannot enter into a church because we have to be changed. NO! We are the church and you can accept God right now with this prayer.

ROMANS 10:9-10 That if thou shalt confess with thy mouth the Lord Jesus, and shalt believe in thine heart that God hath raised him from the dead, thou shalt be saved. For with the heart man believeth unto righteousness; and with the mouth confession is made unto salvation.

2 CORINTHIANS 5:21 For he hath made him to be sin for us, who knew no sin; that we might be made the righteousness of God in him.

HEBREWS 10:25 Not forsaking the assembling of ourselves together, as the manner of some is; but exhorting one another: and so much the more, as ye see the day approaching.

Even when they talked about me, laughed at me, cursed me, tried to run me away from my assignments, I kept coming even more and worshipping even louder, and praising and loving even more and God elevated me because I kept my mind on Jesus and not man, because man didn't give me the ability to have limbs to write this book, man did not give me the knowledge to take the time and patience to write this book to be a blessing to somebody who is carrying burdens and yolk. I come to decree and declare that we don't have to give an account to no-one but JESUS CHRIST OUR SAVIOR!!! And I continue to grow in my ministry to stay in my position as a prayer warrior for those in need and don't understand – that I'm built on a firm foundation. Immovable; steadfast, abounding in the work of the Lord.

1 CORINTHIANS 15:50 Now this I say, brethren, that flesh and blood cannot inherit the kingdom of God; neither doth corruption inherits incorruption.

51 Behold, I shew you a mystery; We shall not all sleep, but we shall all be changed,

52 In a moment, in the twinkling of an eye, at the last trump: for the trumpet shall sound, and the dead shall be raised incorruptible, and we shall be changed.

53 For this corruptible must put on incorruption, and this mortal must put on immortality.

54 So when this corruptible shall have put on incorruption, and this mortal shall have put on immortality, then shall be brought to pass the saying that is written, Death is swallowed up in victory.

55 O death, where is thy sting? O grave, where is thy victory?

56 The sting of death is sin; and the strength of sin is the law.

57 But thanks be to God, which giveth us the victory through our Lord Jesus Christ.

58 Therefore, my beloved brethren, be ye stedfast, unmovable, always abounding in the work of the Lord, forasmuch as ye know that your labour is not in vain in the Lord.

PRAYER: Father, we cannot do this on our own; you did it for me, do it for those that don't know you in the pardon of their sins. Place in their path the right counselor and let them know you are the wonderful counselor. Give my people strength; guide their steps and allow them to walk in the right direction when the temptation of addictions arises.

2 OVERCOMING DIFFICULT TIMES

Most people believe it's essential to know the root of the problem before you can change the circumstances. Maybe some believe it's true, and some believe it's not true. Solutions are new elements that may be injected into some situations, where I have experienced the many difficult times in my life and not knowing that it starts at the root of what you were taught. To be that child of GOD and a praying mother, we still make our own decisions and have to face challenges and difficult times where you just have to learn on your own (or suffer the consequences). I have experienced too many difficult times in my life as a single mother, but through my difficulties, GOD has always been a 'ROCK IN A WEARY LAND'!!! I remember and can recall my son, which is the only son I birthed; when he was 12 years old, I made a decision that I allowed him to live with his dad in another state – which was Indiana. I can relate when they say that experience is the best teaching, but some things I believe a child should not be taught at a certain age. I truly believe a child should not see things and do things at a certain age. Of course, I'm not blaming anyone; so, if you are reading this book, you have to have the wisdom to understand the matter of a mother's concerns and you have to be a mother to even speak on this chapter. So, I advise you to not even continue to read if you don't have a better understanding of a mother or life.

    Well, some background; I was dating Pedro in the eighth grade, then I dated Zeus, which was a Greek guy. My son's father was Zeus's best friend and I would wonder about him before he became my son's father. He would come over to his friend Zeus's house every day, who lived on Beechwood where everyone used to hang out every day by the Beechwood Center where some of the summer jobs were located and where my son's grandparents raised him. I was so in love with Zeus that I wasn't paying my son's father any attention – but trust me – he was madly in love with my sexy bow-legged, light skin with nappy hair. But I kept it laid, and that's what the men liked back then. Well, at least I didn't have a problem with it. So, as time went by, I ended up getting snatch from Zeus and was in the hands of my son's father Big "D". We were high school sweethearts, I loved this man and he loved me, and to this day no-one can separate us from the love of God and the unconditional love we have for one another and the four grandchildren we had.

I remember with my first pregnancy at 15 in the ninth grade, messing with my son's father. I wanted that child so bad, but my mother was like – no we cannot do it, you have potential and you shouldn't be messing with that nappy-headed boy and getting pregnant. But, that's what sneaking does and backing it up with that handsome guy. Now y'all know when I had my son's father, he was the most handsome, best dressing, the sexiest man around the neighborhood.

But, as time went on, I graduated, lived in Big D's mom's house; which they gave me at 18 and spoiled the hell out of me, but I was that female that always kept a career for myself and always kept my head up. I conceived a son, which they called Baby D, and he was Big D's first child and it was truly a blessing when he came into the world. Everybody treated him like a celebrity and spoiled him rotten, so we cannot blame him for who he is today, which he is a great child, very kind, generous, loving, compassionate – but if I had to live it over, I believe he could be a doctor.

As times went on in my life, I experienced difficult times in the relationship with my son's father and it wasn't us - it was the people we allowed in our life. We started dating in 1978 as high-school sweethearts. WOW, a long time ago, right!!! Those were some good old days and times we had, especially being one of the finest/sexiest women in high school and chosen by one of the brothers that all the women wanted. Being that woman where he was a spoiled child, his mom gave me my first house at

18, couldn't tell me anything. He was the best-dressed guy in the seventh grade and his twelfth-grade year, so just imagine the two most popular people dating, it can really cause some difficult times and not only that – some giants and some haters. Now, I look back and see how Jay-Z and Beyoncé and other couples who strived and became multi-millionaires get together and make it to the top. If you don't allow the adversaries to come in, or even if you surround yourself around people that are going down your path.

I remember during our high school years when Big D would cheat with Renee and Rachel and that's how my son had his siblings. We were some fighting females back then, but I am so glad when I look back and how life is already designed; because I love his siblings and they were meant to be. One thing about the difficult times was how us women always fight and want someone else's man. I always was the type of woman of integrity and if I knew someone was taken, I didn't want to be that spare tire. I always was the number one. Now don't get me wrong, I dated men who had other women, but that was after they didn't make it and the man wanted me and that's when the hating really existed. It's strange how I look back over my life and think things over it was some crazy females when it came to my son's father, yeah – he had it going on - but after God delivered me out of the situation and from my praying mother, I realized God had it going on. So, when we broke up, people thought I was crazy because of the money, but baby let me tell you God is a sustainer and the money wasn't worth my life. I was a dog back in the day, I didn't go after men, they all wanted me – because remember, I was that arrogant woman who could have what I wanted, who I wanted and when I wanted it. I was hated on, and I was a hot mess, but I was blessed and I was gorgeous and the men did it to me and I accepted it, of course. I paid for some of the damages we caused in our life, but in the end, I still came out victorious.

Well, my son was conceived on Christmas of 1985 and was born nine months later. A fine, yellow 8lb 5oz son that his dad and everybody in the neighborhood admired and treated him like a celebrity. Well, we were good people, we helped everyone and we just had that gravitating spirit where everyone wanted to hang around us because we had money, lol. Well, the years passed by and his dad went away to college and to become a veterinarian because he loved dogs. I thought I would go to visit him in Bell and Howell where he attended school, he and my cousin Roderick. But two weeks into his experience, he cried to come home to me and his parents. Kaye, Anna Ma, and Big Jim were so disappointed in him. You know when your children drop out of school and you counted on them and believed in them, and they decide to live their own life it does become a hurting thing. So, that's where the generational curse comes from. If the father does it, and then we allow it, the son does it, then their children follow them. But the devil is a liar, it will no longer exist!

Big D was an excellent companion; we traveled the world, we had everything that a couple could have and we knew God. But we weren't following the principles of what we were taught; we wanted to do our own thing and we wanted to live our own lives. So that's when God took his hands off of us, and let us go and that's what happened, but we are still here today because of God's grace. As the years went by, he started cheating with his other baby mother who he had two kids by, and she hated me with a passion. But it wasn't me, it was my man who was a player and decided to have all these women in his life, and when you allow so many spirits in your life and territory it causes disaster and conflict and that's when things get difficult. So basically, being a single mother and my son's father provided for us no matter what the circumstances may have been and he still does today and is the most wonderful dad that a child can have.

Sometimes, we go through a season in our life where we don't even know what choices to take or what direction to go in and that's when you have not matured to the principles of knowing God in a certain way, because once you encounter his supernatural experience and develop a personal relationship, you will know the perfect will of God. Well, allowing my son that opportunity to stay with his father when he was 12, which everyone always said 'let that young man experience that life growing up with his dad', not saying it's a problem – but if you don't have that mother foundation grounded and embedded in that home, the enemy is coming. Now, listening to my adversaries and so-called friends saying in my ear that's his dad, let him go, he is a boy. Yeah! Right. Not that his dad would not protect the environment around his son, the problem was that if you don't know God and weren't rooted and trained in the principles and attributes of knowing God, and even knowing God, but having a personal relationship with God, the environment and your culture will affect you.

From BONDAGE to FREEDOM

PROVERBS 6:20-21 "My son, obey your father's command, and don't neglect your mother's teaching. Keep their words always in your heart, tie them around your neck". ESV

My son in elementary school

Oh! How great is our God? The word is so powerful because that is why my son is still here today because no matter what he faced in life; the word is what will keep you through whatever difficulties you face in life. Experiencing the challenges and allowing him to move to another state at the age of 12 caused the most difficult moments in everyone's lives. He was left to visit one of his dad's friends and the guy's sister who was 16 years old, which us women have that effect on younger guys; because I too loved younger guys and I had the power to manipulate and have what I wanted, because I was all that to men and had that arrogant spirit. So he ended up with an older girl who was beautiful, but wasn't taught the principles of keeping her legs shut; as well as leaving an 12 year-old in the presence of other people who work all the time and never had access to their own home and was not aware of what their children were doing. Don't get me wrong, my readers, but to those that have wisdom, let's be real when we leave our children unattended – the first thing we normally face is child abuse, neglect. That's what the system phrase it to be or become. So, even me being a parent and was brought up with excellent morals and ethics, but it seems even through me not being obedient and not listening can cause an effect on your children. Then it becomes routine and that's where the generational curse continues and someone has to know where it stops. Not to blame his dad or no-one, we just sometimes in our life don't know what choices to take, or just being selfish and doing things our way and we curse our children and we have an effect on our life that sometimes will cost us the rest of our lives.

> ROMANS 12:2 And be not conformed to this world:
> but be ye transformed by the renewing of your mind,
> that ye may prove what is that good, and
> acceptable, and perfect, will of God.

We want to be in the will of God and acceptance of what's good, and that's doing the right thing and listening and letting God perfect us. Now, even though my mother brought her children up in a bible verse church and we were taught the principles of God (Thank God), I was not the perfect daughter. But you learned by keeping the word hidden in your heart so that when you face these difficult times, there was always a shield and a buckler to protect you from those adversaries.

But back to my son - even though his dad allowed him to hang out with one of his son's friends in Indiana, and this particular time frame, he had a sister which was the age of 16 at the time. Imagine your son is 12; now these boys begin to have sex at the age of eight and nine now, which is tremendously ridiculous. My son being this handsome high yellow, fine brother all the women admire to this day, you know him and his dad had it like that (but that's another story there!). My son experienced sex with an older woman and that right there took him to another level, now he ok, he thinks he is grown. Not that we don't want our children to feel like they are in bondage growing up, and mom's always protecting them, but you don't want them to experience issues in their life, where it will affect them the rest of their life either. I was hurt, I was ready to kill his dad and you better believe that when a mother experiences a situation with their kids and people misuse them, you best believe the things that will cross your mind.

To this day I remember my son told me that he would never work for nobody; working check to check and he would never go in the military to get on the front line and get sent to war to die. That's a smart kid back then and he was always full of wisdom. To this day he has his own LLC business; an artist, and never let no-one sign or produce him. And I used to think, 'Son! Come on, let them sign you so I don't have to work anymore' but now everything he makes is his. I'm not saying he is the most perfect man in the world, but I never raised a fool and he never asked anyone for nothing, he was always a soldier with little pride. I can see now why he is the son that fought for his family and for a living because no-one gives you nothing, and even when these young men get caught up in the system not right all the time as well - they use that against you the rest of your life. I have thought about going back to the streets plenty of times; hated on the church, being faithful, family hating, shady jobs... Baby, let me tell you the struggle is real and it not easy staying faithful! But I had to show that example for mine; to let them know there's still a God that sits on the throne waiting on you to come home; was nothing but God's grace that kept me and is keeping my child.

My son is now a successful artist

So, I guess it was that time of my life when my mom and grandparents were casting out imaginations then. Because there was nothing that I couldn't have if I wanted it, especially when it comes to a man that I was attracted to – it can become very dangerous because that gives me the power of control. So, I guess that the young woman took control of my son's body and used that against him. Yeah! I had sex at an early age too, but not 12. That's why us women of God, and even parents if you love your children, be careful with raising them and especially who they are around. The enemy comes to kill, steal, and destroy, and if your children are not rooted in Christ and what you have planted from the foundation is not being used, the enemy will take you and your children out. God knows the plan for our future and it's not for disaster, It's for good.

> *JEREMIAH 29:11 For I know the thoughts that I think toward you, saith the LORD, thoughts of peace, and not of evil, to give you an expected end.*

I remember another difficult time in my life when I started smoking marijuana and we would smoke every day on the way to school, lunch break, after school, and after we go home and finish homework and chores then hit the street and smoke again. I'm quite sure some of us can still relate to this now, but I am so glad I haven't smoked a cigarette or marijuana in over 20 years. Not only did I smoke it, but I also had the best tie stick, skunk, monkey paw, wow – yeah me – we had the best, so that's why I cannot judge the sister that sits next to me on Sunday morning and smells like marijuana. That's why I cannot judge the alcoholic that comes to the altar and smells like he just left the bar, I cannot judge the stripper who just left the strip joint and made $3000 to feed her children and make sure she won't get evicted. Just because we are leaders and worship faithfully, trust me; I come to let you know that my God is as sustainer. I did it all and I still look like God's glory. He is not a respecter God, he loves the just as well as the unjust. If he can save me out of bondage, I believe and trust that he can change you, YES!!! I experienced some difficult times and reminiscing with my mom before she passed and I'm like – I cannot get a whipping now from her, so I shared some things with her. She was so shocked, like where I was at, and how come she didn't know. I would say "Mom, remember, you were praying when I was in my foolishness and God kept me in the cleft of his rock". That's when it goes back to the word.

*PROVERBS 22:6 Train up a child in the way he should
go: and when he is old, he will not depart from it.*

And even when us mothers and parents are praying and trusting God, our children might be doing their own thing and living their life, but trust me; God will snatch them right back out of the enemy's mouth. Thank God somebody prayed for me. It could've been me who strayed and away, been strung out on narcotics and overdosed and never came back. I could've been that drop out of high school early and didn't graduate, but thanks be to God that my son's parents and my parents prayed and God had his hand upon us. We did our dirt and "sinned" but we completed school, so that's why I witness to the dropouts, the ones that strayed and let them know that God is a sustainer, a redeemer, a deliverer, a healer.

*PSALMS 119:67-68 Before I was afflicted I went
astray: but now have I kept thy word. Thou art good,
and doest good; teach me thy statutes.*

Life is full of twists and turns and we may take the wrong path or route but always remember; straight is the gate, and narrow is the path. In my junior year of high school and my senior year, I went to prom with my son's father. I was so favored, my parents and his parents paid for us to go for two years. They did respect the fact that by him being a year older than me, so I still had my last year of high school they allowed him to take me to my senior prom. During the journey, my son's father was a spoiled brother, he drove a fury in the ninth grade and a green LTD that his dad Bobby Lampkin gave him prior to his death in 1979, which was a sad occasion. I really wish my son's siblings could have met that guy (their grandfather). We never had to walk to school, so just imagine that's why everybody would say I was spoiled and I'm still spoiled. I don't look at it like that, I just always had the favor of God upon me. I thank God for always providing!!!

I fought the good fight of faith with my son experiencing the hustling game from generational curses they call it but I come to tell you, you don't know my story when I had to take my savings and me and his dad putting up houses for collateral and fighting case after case after case. Man, oh man! Those were the most difficult times I could ever imagine, your son back and forth in jail like every other week or year. I would just cry out on my knees to God prostrate saying 'God WHY? Why me?" But the Holy Spirit would speak to me saying the same thing; the problem you created will be the same problem you have to endure. People wonder why I became so excellent in praying, and why I am a prayer warrior, and to know that that was my calling all along from the foundation. Every time I would pray, God would answer. Every time I would get closer to God was during the most difficult times, seeing your family six feet under or in jail. And I was like – Lord, whatever you want to do with me, heal my child, protect my child! I was casting down every imagination and stronghold not only for my son but for other people's sons and daughters and family.

I was at the Frank Murphy Hall of Justice on my face; by the elevators on my knees. People thought I was crazy, but we won that battle of a rape case he was accused of; looking at 15 years. I cannot imagine the court days in River Rouge courthouse and the money we spent bonding him out of jail. It had got to a point where I was representing cases for him, and for my nephews and friends. The power I had that God had given me, wherever I was stepping and the soles of my feet were holding down scorpions, lions and serpents and people were so amazed like "how is he out?".

Baby, let me tell you to God be the glory and his grace is sufficient. You can call me what you want, but I learned to trust him and my worship is real and he is a prayer-answering God. I remember when he caught a rape case and the attorney was a deacon and one of the best attorneys in Michigan and I recalled a lot of people saying 'he going down', 'he about to do 15 years for rape' not knowing God was whispering in my ear saying he didn't do it. I just rest assured that when I walked into the courtroom, my son was going home.

Then, I had to get real with it. How is it that these men were catching so many rape cases? Not trying to protect my son, but the evidence from the medical tests showed that my son's accuser hadn't been touched by him. The most difficult time of that season was our own friends and family arguing with me and said he won't beat that case. So, we still won the victory. Because people say they trust GOD, but do you really trust him when your back is up against the wall and you are not knowing what the outcome will be, but let me tell you – say what you want about ME. Yes! People laughed, said I was crazy, lied on us, but I kept the faith and my trust till this day is built on nothing less than JESUS CHRIST AND HIS RIGHTEOUSNESS!!! And the same ones that laughed to this day, I pray for their families and lost ones. How can you say you love a God you never seen, but cannot love, speak, encourage or stand by your family and friends through difficult times?

THE DEVIL IS A LIAR!!!

If we stop putting ourselves in situations, we won't have a rape case or we won't be doing life in the penitentiary, because we have to be wise and make the right decisions in life. Then, we may ask "What's the right decision?" Knowledge to go to school, knowledge you get in a bible vs. church and be taught the principles and instructions of who God truly is, and he will keep you if you continue to walk with him. We as men and women don't have to jump in bed or put ourselves in situations just because the woman or man is so attractive to you. We have to learn that sometimes God can be using us as an instrument to be a blessing to someone else and we are thinking 'this the one' or 'this my man or husband', but we have to pray for wisdom and take heed as to what we are getting ourselves into. That's why the divorce rate is so high and we are not making it in these relationships. There have been times in life, dealing with my nephews - one I can recall who had about three murder cases who I let come live with me – just being Auntie who always thought no matter what they go through, no-one's perfect. I'm still Auntie and I love you no matter what. Now, don't get me wrong – he did the time, so we cannot hold that against them when they have served their time. Only God can judge you!

Now, this nephew would hide guns in the house and one day, my son at five years old found the gun, wooooh!!! Thanks be to God he didn't shoot himself, or me. It's people's children that take guns to school, shoot family members, kill their parents at a heartbeat, but thanks be to God we were covered in the blood of the lamb. I have to take a praise break there – HALLELUJAH!!!! Another nephew, my baby Chilly is doing a bit for murder, and the guy that was killed was a son of a man I used to date and he loved me, and we came to court with tears in our eyes. Yes, his son was dead and my nephew was looking at life. It's always two sides to a story, but the commandment speaks on thou shall not kill, so what do you do when people constantly pick with you and come in your house to rob you or disrespect you? Well, I come to tell you there were killings in the bible. Who says it was right? No-one can judge us but God.

> *GENESIS 7:23 And every living substance was destroyed which was upon the face of the ground, both man, and cattle, and the creeping things, and the fowl of the heaven; and they were destroyed from the earth: and Noah only remained alive, and they that were with him in the ark.*

> *GENESIS 19:24 Then the LORD rained upon Sodom and upon Gomorrah brimstone and fire from the LORD out of heaven;*

> *GENESIS 19:26 But his wife looked back from behind him, and she became a pillar of salt.*

> *EXODUS 7:15 Get thee unto Pharaoh in the morning; lo, he goeth out unto the water; and thou shalt stand by the river's brink against he come; and the rod which was turned to a serpent shalt thou take in thine hand.*

> *16 And thou shalt say unto him, The LORD God of the Hebrews hath sent me unto thee, saying, Let my people go, that they may serve me in the wilderness: and, behold, hitherto thou wouldest not hear.*

> *17 Thus saith the LORD, In this thou shalt know that I am the LORD: behold, I will smite with the rod that is in mine hand upon the waters which are in the river, and they shall be turned to blood.*

18 And the fish that is in the river shall die, and the river shall stink; and the Egyptians shall lothe to drink of the water of the river.

19 And the LORD spake unto Moses, Say unto Aaron, Take thy rod, and stretch out thine hand upon the waters of Egypt, upon their streams, upon their rivers, and upon their ponds, and upon all their pools of water, that they may become blood; and that there may be blood throughout all the land of Egypt, both in vessels of wood, and in vessels of stone.

20 And Moses and Aaron did so, as the LORD commanded; and he lifted up the rod, and smote the waters that were in the river, in the sight of Pharaoh, and in the sight of his servants; and all the waters that were in the river were turned to blood.

21 And the fish that was in the river died; and the river stank, and the Egyptians could not drink of the water of the river; and there was blood throughout all the land of Egypt.

22 And the magicians of Egypt did so with their enchantments: and Pharaoh's heart was hardened, neither did he hearken unto them; as the LORD had said.

23 And Pharaoh turned and went into his house, neither did he set his heart to this also.

24 And all the Egyptians digged round about the river for water to drink; for they could not drink of the water of the river.

25 And seven days were fulfilled, after that the LORD had smitten the river.

EXODUS 12:29-30 And it came to pass, that at midnight the LORD smote all the firstborn in the land of Egypt, from the firstborn of Pharaoh that sat on his throne unto the firstborn of the captive that was in the dungeon; and all the firstborn of cattle. And Pharaoh rose up in the night, he, and all his servants, and all the Egyptians; and there was a great cry in Egypt; for there was not a house where there was not one dead.

EXODUS 17:13 And Joshua discomfited Amalek and his people with the edge of the sword.

JOSHUA 10:26 And afterward Joshua smote them, and slew them, and hanged them on five trees: and they were hanging upon the trees until the evening.

Now, I can go on and on about killings in biblical days. Again, not saying it's right, but only God knows and I truly believe it's the situation you put yourself in and the life choices you make. I'm glad through all the difficult times I experienced, and carrying guns at a young age, and being in the worldly thing, I thank God he kept my conscience and my sanity to not retaliate and take revenge into my own hands. Being realistic, I have thought about it once upon a time, but the Holy Spirit will convict you and you have to take control of your thoughts and cast down every imagination that arises. I'm not trying to be that theologian and explain why people kill, or why it happened in biblical times as well as happening on a daily basis today among our own generation and culture. That's something we would have to take to God and learn to serve God, so we cannot put ourselves in these situations. And people, that comes back to how you raise your children and their upkeep, and how us mothers have to continue to feed and minister that word to our children from birth. Because we are all were born in sin from the first. Adam and God gave us a comforter to sustain us and gave us the chance to be converted from our old ways so that we can become new creatures and live in newness.

As time went on, through my difficult times, not regretting none of it, it was just a learning experience. I made a choice to work as a bartender for three years and I made more money than working at Ford Motor Company and just because I wasn't a stripper in the bar, I still was part of it and I was getting stripped from my dignity and integrity of what my mother planted. Don't get me wrong – now remember, we make our own choices. I'm just an instrument and a disciple being used for the kingdom to let my women and even men know that there is always a greater calling. There is nothing wrong with working in certain environments, but if you don't know God and have the faith, or a praying family and was rooted – you might not make it out of the bar, you might not make it out of the strip club, you might not make it out of the dope game. So why put ourselves in a situation just because the money was good? Money is the root of all evil, and it will take you straight to hell.

> *1 TIMOTHY 6:9-10 But they that will be rich fall into temptation and a snare, and into many foolish and hurtful lusts, which drown men in destruction and perdition. For the love of money is the root of all evil: which while some coveted after, they have erred from the faith, and pierced themselves through with many sorrows.*

Money can become dangerous and the reason for that is the same reason loaded guns are dangerous; they can both be used only by one kind of people – fallen sinners. Money is like a loaded gun; it can destroy you and your family. The desire is the love of money, where everyone wants to get rich.

The love of money can be a deliberate decision or a desire that has not been thought through carefully. People have their minds and goals set to be this multi-millionaire or trillionaire to enjoy the lifestyle but are as miserable as ever. We can lack contentment, which is not having the purpose or the perspective of eternity or knowing GOD himself. So, people let's not lust for the things of this world but be ye transformed by the renewing of our mind.

Not renewing our mind and making our own choices, working in the bar, money-getting people. I only hung with the ones who had money, if you didn't have money, wasn't no hanging out with Liz! Oh yeah, we partied and we had the best time of our life, but leaving the club at 3am in the wee hours of the night, traveling by myself sometimes, or rolling with my hustling buddy Crystal, one of my ride or die girls that I can trust, that had my back. I remember a guy did a drive-by and killed a guy right in front of the door of the club. That hustling life required some hardship – trust me, I'm a living witness. Then, I remember about 4am in the morning leaving the club, me and my ace boon coon Crystal, we were high as a kite and the vehicle stopped on us when her man told us not to take that car that night. So, we were stranded on mack on the freeway. Come on, eastside in the 80's on the freeway at 3am in the morning. Yeah! There was God with us, his name is 'Emmanuel'. God is with us!

2 THESSALONIANS 3:3 But the Lord is faithful, who shall stablish you, and keep you from evil.

We were stranded on the freeway and a guy (angel) not knowing at that time had stopped behind us, and man, we were scared, but he ended up giving us a ride home and we come to find out the guy was disabled with no legs. Of course, you know me – I had to wrestle with the enemy at first and baby we were going down together. We had gasoline and lighters in the truck plotting to burn this guy up if he tried anything. Oh!!! I was a gangster, I didn't play. But while I made good money in the bar, and was a magnet for any brother I wanted, I wasn't happy within me. You know they called women players back then because I always had a man and he was there picking me up on those days; it was my life-long lover Mike. I worked, so God always covered me under his wings. One thing about my lifestyle - I was a woman that probably ran my mouth, but I was a grateful woman. I might not have understood and didn't appreciate everything, but I shared everything I had with somebody. I didn't understand what favor was, but today growing in Christ and knowing God from the foundation of my ancestor "favor just ain't fair" because God has given me unmerited, immeasurable favor. Over my entire life, people will hate you from the favor of God upon you. God is an awesome God. Yes, I had my own place at 18 years old and took care of my parents. I recall a difficult time when my nephew used to put guns under my son's bed and he was playing with it and I happened to look up and discover it. Oh my GOD!!! Did I nut up on my nephew, Taurus! Well, well, well, it's a whole new world and generation out here; these teenagers are selfish. Don't want to help their parents and if they do, it's not from the heart. The world's treatment of its children is a formula for spoiling; enabling selfish human beings, and selfishness becomes more dominant the older a person becomes. That's why we as parents have to teach our children from the foundation to honor and respect your parents and respect others.

But sometimes we as adults step out when we turn 18 and want to experience that grown life, and if we are not equipped or instructed, we fall right back to your parent's pad (home)!!! "Train up a child in the way they shall be and they will never depart". I thank God for my parents and my mother being a soldier in the army of the Lord, because even through our mistakes, and being wet behind the ears and testing our waters, we were covered in the blood and there was a covenant over us while we were in our foolishness. I pray and believe that same grace that was on our ancestors, is the same grace that covers us today. We can rest assured in the fact and know that God is always faithful, even when we didn't understand and was disobedient to our task; God still reigned and covered us.

> *COLOSSIANS 1:10 "He delivered us from such a deadly peril, and he will deliver us. On him we have set our hope that he will deliver is again." ESV*

> *COLOSSIANS 1:13 "He has delivered us from the domain of darkness and transferred us to the kingdom of his beloved son." ESV*

I remember when my son was 21 and he was in the hood, well; he had just left the house and wasn't gone 10 minutes. In front of my brother's house and he was thrown on top of the police vehicle and arrested. Taken in – found with a few so-called ecstasy pills. Now, from the time he got arrested and got to the station and me and his dad get the lawyer and go to bond him out, he suddenly had 10 pills of ecstasy on him, which carries 10 years for one pill. Plus, a $600,000 bond! Now, we already had the mentality of being lawyers, judges, prosecutors. Me and his dad were very intelligent, now if you are going to set him up, you had to come correct. God says what the devil meant for evil, he will turn it into good. So, we waited out the 72 hours. So, they can send him to county - of course, it tore me up – but baby, by the three days I prayed, now the three days is when God was resurrected. And his dad and I got to the courts, the bond was down to $600.00. There is a God that sits on the throne.

Abraham and Moses failed. Peter, and Paul and also David failed, but God used their failures to carry out his will.

PRAYER: Lord we all have sinned and have fallen short of your glory. I came to you Lord when I failed, and you picked me up; so, let your people know that you love them just as well as the unjust. Lord, all our failures lead us back to you and repentance. Lord, if we are always a winner in the race and journey of life, we wouldn't have to rely on you; that's where your mercy endures. So, I thank you that when we fall your unchanging hands and arms are always there to carry and pick us up.

3 OVERCOMING LIFE CHALLENGES

Without life, there would not be life challenges and without dealing with and facing challenges of life there will not be success and overcoming what we have to master to be who we are. One season in my life that I can say was one of the most difficult challenges; I was going back to college at the age of 35 and challenging the most difficult studies which were Microbiology, Anatomy, Pharmacology, Medical Terminology, Psychology. I remember when I lost my job at Ford Motor Company when the big three crashed and everyone was so terrified and leaving the States, jobs were transferred out of the country and Bush was the President and it was so chaotic. But one thing that I can say to this day, no matter who was in office, no matter what challenges I had or we had to challenge, I made it through because we know that God does his best work in the midst of chaotic situations.

    I can recall in 2001 when I had suffered for years with my gallbladder and knew the situation and was scared to have it removed, it was flared up and poisoned, not even knowing through my suffering season, God was already preparing me for his greatness and to go into the medical field. So, this particular day, which was September 11th, 2001 – which we still have that special day on 9/11 which was so terrifying even when we look back and see the loved ones and the soldiers that had fought for our country and people so devastated. Well, that particular morning I was scheduled for surgery to get my gallbladder removed. I had made the appointment, went through with it without fear, so that was another fear that I had conquered. Early that morning, waiting for my sister to come and pick me up - who forgot about me - so the enemy wanted me to change the surgery appointment. But I prayed and trusted God and drove myself to the hospital, now that's a praise break right there!

Praise God for keeping me!!!

I had to be at the hospital at approximately 6am. Surgery was scheduled at 7am, and as I approached the admitting area and following instructions where the wheelchair took me to the surgery room for prepping, I was like; Oh, here I go! I always did it on my own and by the grace of God and his mercy. I got down to pre-operative suite and as they were checking my vital signs and getting ready to give me local anesthetic for surgery – everything just changed in the twinkle of an eye. I saw Doctors and Nurses and staff running in and I'm a little drowsy from the anesthesia, so I'm just at peace and no-one's telling me what's going on, but of course, I had the Holy Spirit guiding me to be still and I recognized something wasn't right. Next thing I know, I was in my room after surgery, my dad had ordered phone and tv services so all I can see are planes hitting a building. I thought nothing of it because I was still nauseous and drowsy from the medication. The nurses didn't want to tell me what was going on because they didn't want to upset me or have me leaving the hospital worried about what was happening, and it's a matter of fact there wasn't nothing I could do. When my sister Sally (she picked up my daughter who was 10 years old at that time) and they came to the hospital and told me what was going on, that we had been under attack and the twin towers and the Pentagon had been attacked and there was nothing I could do but pray. I was sore, I couldn't move, I was wondering where my son, Baby D was at. He's my only son and the Lord told me to be still and know that it's God, that he had him. He was hanging out as usual, not worried about nothing. So, going through that challenge of my life – it was a big challenge in my life – just as well as others.

As the years went by and people were losing jobs, car industry jobs were sent overseas, it was a disaster and a famine in the land for a long time. And what I'm getting to is that sometimes in our life, through our biggest and hardest challenges, God still brings the good out of it. I was a traffic inbound and outbound dispatcher for Ford Motor Company and I was also working for Penske logistics making great money, which I was always blessed with good jobs and great opportunities, but somehow, I would always get knocked back for some particular reason. And that's the meaning of challenges, the challenges and obstacles we face in life are what brings the best out of us and success if we don't faint. You know the meaning of challenges is a call to take part in a contest or competition, especially a duel. So basically, the challenge is either you win or you lose. A challenge is something that by nature or character serves as a call to battle.

> MATTHEW 16:24-26 Then said Jesus unto his disciples, If any man will come after me, let him deny himself, and take up his cross, and follow me. For whosoever will save his life shall lose it: and whosoever will lose his life for my sake shall find it. For what is a man profited, if he shall gain the whole world, and lose his own soul? or what shall a man give in exchange for his soul?

So, we face all types of challenges in our lives, but are we going to deny ourselves or pick up the cross and follow Jesus and stay on the battlefield and continue to face life challenges? So that we can go to the next higher dimension and get to see the glory of who God really is, or are we going to complain like the man at the pool for 38 years and miss out on our dreams and purpose that's pre-destined from the foundation?

> JOHN 5:1 After this there was a feast of the Jews; and Jesus went up to Jerusalem.
>
> 2 Now there is at Jerusalem by the sheep market a pool, which is called in the Hebrew tongue Bethesda, having five porches.
>
> 3 In these lay a great multitude of impotent folk, of blind, halt, withered, waiting for the moving of the water.

4 For an angel went down at a certain season into the pool, and troubled the water: whosoever then first after the troubling of the water stepped in was made whole of whatsoever disease he had.

5 And a certain man was there, which had an infirmity thirty and eight years.

6 When Jesus saw him lie, and knew that he had been now a long time in that case, he saith unto him, Wilt thou be made whole?

7 The impotent man answered him, Sir, I have no man, when the water is troubled, to put me into the pool: but while I am coming, another steppeth down before me.

8 Jesus saith unto him, Rise, take up thy bed, and walk.

9 And immediately the man was made whole, and took up his bed, and walked: and on the same day was the sabbath.

10 The Jews therefore said unto him that was cured, It is the sabbath day: it is not lawful for thee to carry thy bed.

11 He answered them, He that made me whole, the same said unto me, Take up thy bed, and walk.

12 Then asked they him, What man is that which said unto thee, Take up thy bed, and walk?

13 And he that was healed wist not who it was: for Jesus had conveyed himself away, a multitude being in that place.

14 Afterward Jesus findeth him in the temple, and said unto him, Behold, thou art made whole: sin no more, lest a worse thing come unto thee.

15 The man departed, and told the Jews that it was Jesus, which had made him whole.

Don't get me wrong, for the ones who don't understand the knowledge of following Christ of course if we are not born-again, and have not accepted Christ as our personal savior, we don't know what it is to pick up the cross. But if we learned to understand the true meaning of Christ, the son of God who died on the cross for our sins and so that we will have eternal life; then we should understand the true meaning of what Christ carried. He carried all of our burdens and our sins, so why do we get depressed and have anxiety issues and doubt and worry when he paid the price and we don't have to do anything but live and enjoy our journey? So, it goes back to my challenge of losing my job when the big three crashed because of the enemy that attacked us and it not only affected me, it affected the whole nation, but we got through it. After I was laid off at Ford, I went to God and I said:

"Daddy - where do I go, what do I do?"

And I fasted, I trusted him and he told me to go back to school and I said:

"GO BACK TO SCHOOL?!"

Like the man at the pool, I was complaining - telling the creator it's people younger than me and will make it before me; or they are smarter than me, and that's what kept me in bondage so long. Not believing in myself and listening to the wrong people that didn't want to achieve, and wanted to keep you in bondage as well. But again, I come to tell you that we are never too old to accomplish God's purpose and plan; and he will give you life, exceedingly and more abundantly than we can ever ask or imagine. But listen; it's according to the "POWER" that works within us.

We have AUTHORITY; DOMINION AND POWER to work that thang!

I'm like – go back to school? The enemy was making me think I was too old and he was trying to play tricks on my mind and I had to stand up against the wiles of the enemy and let him know I was wonderfully and fearfully made in the image of God. It's nothing too hard for God and I have the power to do it. So, I got up and went to WCCCD and I registered for classes in 2005 of August and I was a 4.0 honor student every semester and graduated with an Associates of Applied Science Degree of Surgical Technology in December of 2009. It was another challenge because now I had to go to work by doing my externship at a hospital in Dearborn. I was scheduled through my professor who was a Russian, a great man and he helped me tremendously and worked as a Surgeon for over 45 years. He wasn't aware that his staff would be prejudiced towards me being the only black woman in the operating room. At the time there was another black girl, but she had been working there for over 10 years and was half white; so that was a challenge getting out in the real world of the high demand fields and accomplishing a great accomplishment and now I have to deal with bigger giants. Now they say 'the bigger the level the bigger the devil' and it is so true. I was set up in my last week after 15 weeks of externship one of the white girls who had been my preceptor and was so nice to me but was stabbing me behind my back all the time. And I came to find out she had never been to school, she was hired through who she knew, and being the color that she was, but it was all well with God. So, not knowing when you go to school and get a high-demand degree you become intimidating to the other staff who do not have the knowledge and the education but have the experience. So, now I'm experiencing the real world of how it goes back to the scripture.

> *EPHESIANS 6:12 For we wrestle not against flesh and blood, but against principalities, against powers, against the rulers of the darkness of this world, against spiritual wickedness in high places.*

So, the last week of my externship when the manager was going to hire me; they advised me to submit my resume and credentials. But she pushed the sterile table against me in the OR and lied and said I contaminated her field after the surgery was over. I didn't know anything until the next day - so they didn't hire me - and it affected me for over a year, and if you don't get hired within your externship it will affect you in the future for the hiring process. I didn't understand it then, but now I can look back over the challenges I faced and give God the glory because even though it didn't work out for the good back then he had a greater plan for me. I continued to apply for jobs in Michigan and I was going through a rejection season for over nine months. And I never gave up, even though I got hired at a hospital in Ann Arbor - I took a lower-paying job in the operating room as a Central Sterile Processor. The hiring RN manager told me that after six months I could apply for a surgical tech role, which is what I went to school for; and they would use me as a shared services position where I could still work for the other job, plus in the operating room. During the process of the position becoming available, they ended up hiring another white girl in my place so I still continued to press toward the mark of the most-high, God. Crying and on my face prostrate every day, and God was humbling me and showing me the fruits of the spirit, which was self-control, love, peace, generosity, and joy. To tell you the truth, I was getting frustrated and it was a very hopeless situation. But instead of letting the enemy destroy me, I continued to be the greater warrior in battle, I became a fighter in the spirit and it got worse and worse and worse. I was then approved to go to another hospital after speaking to my professors about the situation and letting them know I went to school, accomplished my goals, and this is what I get?

They paid liability insurance and let me do another externship. I went into the operating room at another hospital for 10 weeks; never was late, didn't miss a day, specialized and scrubbed every case that I was trained for and here comes the next giant. My supervisor was a black woman that I had spoken to about my situation and asked her can she help me out? She told me to get my resume that they would be hiring - and it was four positions. I was challenged with the doctors, and one of the best heart specialists who had trained me in hearts and I was great in that area was supposed to sit on the panel the day of my interview. The manager pulled him off the panel when it was my time to interview and they gave all four positions to white girls; so, it doesn't matter what race, ethics, color we are all just as prejudiced against our own race. That right there blew my mind because you hear about these things, my dad experienced it 80 years ago and it still exists. It's one of the most devastating challenges a person can experience when you know you're doing the right thing and the enemy tries to take it from you. That's why to this day I know how to go in the trenches and pray. I have learned how to take back everything the enemy has stolen, but to have to challenge your own race and go through jealousy and intimidation because you decided to make up your mind to use the gift and talents God ordained for me when I was in my mother's womb, and then the devil tries to take it, he is a liar. It showed me how to stay in my word even more - to go to church even more and receive what God has for me. I didn't give up, I didn't give in. I kept pressing toward the mark of the most-high God, which is Jesus.

PRAYER: Lord God, DAVID was a young kid that they doubted, but he took a slingshot and killed a giant; not with his expertise, but with your strength. Lord God, I don't want to be on the frontline fighting a battle without you as my commander. Lord, continue to equip your people through life challenges as we stay on the battlefield.

4 OVERCOMING FRUSTRATION

Studying the field of psychology as I researched cognitive areas of my life, I came across the truth of knowing that frustration is a form of poorly expressed anger. Well, anger can become dangerous which is an emotion characterized by antagonism toward someone or something you feel has deliberately done you wrong. Sometimes anger can be a good thing; which is another form of psychological aspect where it can give you a way to express negative feelings for example, or motivate you to find solutions to problems. Now, when it comes to excessive anger, that's when it can become dangerous or a huge problem far as an increase in high blood pressure and other physical changes that can affect you to think straight or even other mental issues.

There was a season in my life where I went through a very angry and frustrating period in my life of transition. I had accepted Christ and was being converted to a new creature in Christ and that was putting old things behind me and pressing toward the mark of the most-high GOD which is in Christ Jesus. It's amazing how God can change anyone, and I know that if he can change me, he can change anybody. As time went on in my life, taking a step of faith every day, focusing on the plan that God had for me, and making a decision to do the right things in life; like taking a faith walk and going back to school at the age of 40 and accomplishing my goals and following my purpose it really became a very, very frustrating time of my life. I had to make a decision after the big three crashed working as a traffic inbound clerk for the logistic department for Ford Motor Company, a customer service coordinator and also a Ford recall representative. Of course, it was a good job making top dollar, but not expecting the economy to crash during that time. Now remember it's not my will, but I'm thinking it was. That is why we have to keep our hope and trust in Christ because you never know what to expect the next minute. 'Nothing is promised to no-one!'

God is our source and the jobs are just a resource that he lets us use temporarily while we here on earth for a short time. Getting pregnant at the age of 30 years old with my daughter; which disappointed my mother and father, when they thought so highly of me...they thought that I would go off to college or to the air-force where I had always dreamt, and I allowed my dreams to die at that time and made my own choices and met my daughter's dad which that spirit of lust took over me, WOW!!! Very frustrating, but I never regret her as a daughter, a very proud mother today. But I never thought that he would walk out of her life at the age of eight years old because we couldn't make it. Her dad figured if he couldn't have me, he didn't want neither one of us. I couldn't ever understand that, but dating a guy that was 10 years younger than me (and he lied about his age from day one) and I trusted him because he was that fine, sexy, young brother can become a very frustrating situation if you are not mindful or don't have the wisdom of what life is really about. You have to pray for wisdom. It's a gift that God gives you, and it will lead you and direct you to the right aspect of choices and decisions in life and I just didn't have it at that time. But I thank God that he has delivered me out of the mouth of the enemy and I received the gift of wisdom.

LUKE 21:15 For I will give you a mouth and wisdom, which all your adversaries shall not be able to gainsay nor resist.

God still remains to be a father to the fatherless and she never wanted for nothing having me as a mother. He has tried to establish that relationship with her but she is an adult and she chooses not to; and to be honest, that is the most frustrating situation in my life. When God uses you and you have to bow and do what God tells you to do no matter how angry you are because he is the only one that can fix it, you might as well be obedient.

I'm the kind of woman that still gives those that messed up and sold me out, the benefit of the doubt. And I see the good in people and that's how Christ is…for example, my daughter's father. She hates when I would and still today protect him; he was there for 9 years of her life; was a barber making bucks on the eastside and would catch buses and walk miles to feed us and make sure she had what she needed. I can feel her pain and understand the hurt of him not being there for her high school years and certain times of a daughter's life, but we have to still give God thanks in all things. I truly know that's why she and I are so close to this day; we were all each other had through those struggling years of being a single parent, but I come to tell the world we never wanted for nothing and never will. When she had a battle with her girlfriends it was my battle and will fight a bear for mines and still will today.

Well, anyway, being a single mom raising my daughter Niq on my own wasn't easy – the journey was challenging, but God brought us through. Having to drop her off at the age of six and seven years of age at daycare not knowing if you were going to see your child again, not being able to function at work worried about if your child is ok and not seeing your baby until 7pm at night five days a week. Women or even single dads monitor and do some background checks on who you are dating and what you are getting yourself into when you are starting a relationship. I'm not saying that all men and women are not the perfect matches but when my parents were raising us, we had fathers in the household at least one parent was there to raise us if the other was working and that's the reason why life is so frustrating for us single parents; struggling and raising children on our own because of the choices we make in life. Why should we have to work, cook, clean, and manage everything when God gave men the authority to take care of your responsibilities? Even if we had children out of wedlock, it doesn't mean you should be deadbeat fathers or even women leaving their children for the men to be responsible for. We laid down and had them together so I believe that we should go through the same struggle together.

Through the years of me being a single mom, it made me to be the strongest, most phenomenal example, not only to my daughter but to other single mothers and my daughter's friends who would call me mom. They had mothers, but they weren't nurturing mothers. So, life might become frustrating, but it always brings the good out of bad situations. My daughter never missed a meal; dressed the best and was an excellent straight "A" student and graduated in the first semester of her senior year. Because of her stickler and nurturing, praying mother that did it by herself and God's grace and mercy. She is also my event planner who takes care of all my business and it's not easy trusting everyone, but I'm a proud mother to have raised her on my own and she turned out to be excellent without any children being 25 praise God. I'm praying and interceding now for twins and her future husband.

Despite the challenges, my daughter grew into a strong young woman

My pastor's a very dedicated man to God and 95% of the people that he married are still together. Of course, you are going to go through hardship and challenges in marriage, because it's a covenant and it's sacred, the devil doesn't want that. But one thing I can say; if you try marital counseling it will work every time because you are spending quality time and getting your matters and most of your problems out there before you jump up and tie the knot.

> *PHILLIPPIANS 4:6 Be careful for nothing; but in every thing by prayer and supplication with thanksgiving let your requests be made known unto God.*

We have to pray without ceasing people, and that's to constantly pray before you make any decision in life and to petition yourself to God. Make your voice be known, let God hear you cry, your request and then pray for a spiritual eye and an attentive ear to hear what thus said the Lord before you make a choice. But I can truly say God kept me and I seem to manage though my frustrating choices and I just wasn't giving up on my dream or what God had planned for me even though I raised children on my own and made my own choices in life. You know – living out in Brownstown and Woodhaven in a very suburban area and of course I'm quite sure you can relate to that and the challenges and frustrations I had to deal with, where people would say "this is the white neighborhood" or "why are all the black people moving this way, people need to learn to stop living a lie" and in a stereotyped world where people believe that they own a city or country.

WE DON'T OWN NOTHING.

Ok, let me take you back to the word.

> *2 CORINTHIANS 4:18 While we look not at the things which are seen, but at the things which are not seen: for the things which are seen are temporal; but the thing which are not seen are eternal.*

So, this particular passage takes us back to everything belongs to God, and I can care less about what's temporal; my soul is anchored in Christ and salvation. If we learn to get off our high horses and stop being in competition and trying to please the world and please God, we can go very far in life and he will give us the desires of our heart. Even though living in a neighborhood of self-righteous folk and the challenges and frustration I face every day as a black African American woman, I still overcame my obstacles and continue to stand on the word of God and achieve my goals in spite of it all. It's time for unity and to stop limiting our expectations to where we can or cannot live. Well, well, well - I lived downriver for over 12 years and I succeeded, and anywhere you live it's what you make out of it and how you keep your neighborhood together and what to expect for the future of the next generation. What's the saying? We don't take the people out of the ghetto; we take the ghetto out of the neighborhood.

I remember a very frustrating season where one of my managers, a black brother high authority position who would favor me every day, he would give me all the overtime; let me leave early and always would still give me my time. Now, come on - me being young and not wise, smart but not wise, thought I was all that you know – a gorgeous brick house woman that all the men wanted; right! They wanted my sex and caused nothing but disaster and frustration in my life; being that woman of manipulating power and can look at a man and get what I wanted. Don't get me wrong – I still can today, but I've been converted and I choose Christ and not man. Because in order to receive the blessing and miracles of God you have to change, you have to be converted, you have to ask God to create in you a new heart and a right spirit so that you can recognize the wiles and fiery darts of the enemy because baby, he comes in all kinds of packages! If it wasn't for the Lord on my side where would I be? You know in life no matter what we do in the dark it's coming to light and you are going to have to repeat itself until you get it right. So why not practice a daily walk with God and go the long ride and not short cut yourself because you are only making it worse for you and what God has in store for you. Yeah!!! I was smart, but thinking since the brother like me, I can work him. And yeah, the money was great but I ended losing a great job. Of course, women, sisters who are reading this chapter; you know you can relate to where I'm coming from. We were not always converted and 'HOLY THOU ART'!!! All of our life we all have some secrets and skeletons in the closet. We know frustration is a form of poorly expressed anger. I was angry, not with losing, but having to go back to school at the age of 40 not knowing I was frustrated for nothing and it was already predestined in God's plan. We don't know the plan, but we have to be instructed and ask God for insight and direction to lead us into his perfect will. Not our will but "GOD'S WILL BE DONE"!!!

Even through the setbacks and frustrations in our life, we decide to make a difference in our lives and find our purpose; here come those adversaries. After losing my job I woke up one morning and I had a little talk with Jesus. I ask God at this point after I repented, I said: "At my age, after all the time and effort I put into working and building my 401K retirement and accomplishing goals, what is going on?!" God spoke to me in 2005 and he told me to go back to school and start over - it's never too late no matter how old you get. Trust me, with my smart mouth questioning God and I said "Why God? What do you mean, go back to school?"

I was living good in a fabulous townhouse in Brownstown making good money thought I was set for life... but that wake-up call! I may have been overlooked and looked over or just going through the motions of frustration and rejection, but isolation is a reservation period of uncertainty and just a set-up of the mind reservation of what God is preparing for your greatness. When God gets ready to claim what's his, there will always be opposition. So, I had to overcome the spirit of frustration, not because of what I went through, but because of what I allowed myself to go through. The awesome experience is going through the fire and knowing that GOD is fireproof and you might go through some pain and suffering, but you want to get burnt and you are coming out as pure gold.

Now, my daughter is a 4.0 student attending school and working making bucks as a waitress with great tips and ministering to the young women who have children with no fathers. She also served for years at Union Grace Missionary Baptist Church in the nursery and she has established a work environment to nurture children. So, we look back over our lives and wonder why we go through things, but what the devil meant for evil, God turns it into the good and she took what she didn't get and put it back into someone else's life and that's what ministry is. Don't revenge on others or take things out on people because of the frustration and obstacles we have experienced in life. Let's learn to turn someone else's situation around and show the love of God so that the kingdom can advance through our love and God's grace.

We made it through together, as a team!

PRAYER: Lord God, JAMES 1:19-20 says be quick to listen and slow to speak. Lord, there was a time when I didn't understand the passage, but thanks to your understanding and being in your will I've learned; Lord God teach your people that might not understand to not be so temper-headed when we get frustrated with the things we cannot have when we want it. My frustration will never produce your righteousness; Lord your righteousness is everything! Please Lord allow it to be transformed in your people's hearts.

5 OVERCOMING GOSSIPING

You know we have all been through a season in our lives when we just had nothing to do, being immature people who just have to GOSSIP! I would've never known in my immature stages, that I'd wish I could take back all the gossip that I presented to others. But the saying is 'never regret what you been through, it's just a lesson learned'. You know to gossip is the exaggeration or fabrication of a story, regarding somebody other than the talebearer, in the absence of this person who is being discussed for the malicious purpose of demeaning. What are you going to accomplish out of speaking rumors; whispering, slandering or tarnishing the person's reputation?

MATTHEW says we must present ourselves as adults. When we were kids, we talk like kids, but now we are adults, so I come to present the transition of being free from BONDAGE to FREEDOM that God has fulfilled in my life. We, as grown women and men sometimes in our life we just need to mind our own business and mostly stay out of everybody else's. GOD has matured me out of the enemies' mouth for himself to use me as his willing vessel to save a dying world.

It's a wonderful privilege in life when you know you have been transfigured and become a new creature in Christ. To be around that gossip; it just eats at your spirit. You know when you are born again when you start to be convicted of your old mindset and no longer be so judgmental and work on your own faults, but you just cannot evolve yourself in the presence of gossipers and negative vibes any longer. What is so amazing about being transformed from being a gossiper is when you can encourage another individual to speak positive and encourage the next individual. Instead of always trying to put a person beneath you, or even being around old friends who have not changed, and not including yourself or agreeing with gossip...oh, that's when they really start gossiping and talking about how holy you are! But, let me tell you something - Jesus is holy, so if you are walking with Christ you become set aside from the gossiping and negative people and you want to be just like Christ.

I love the song Marvin Sapp sings, which is one of my favorites, that 'when others seen the worst in me my GOD seen the best' !!! That's one thing about being converted in Christ - get ready for the ride! The enemy doesn't see change in the next individual, because they continue to live in bondage and the scales are covering their eyes; so they're blind and cannot see what you see, because you are walking in the "SUPERNATURAL" not the "NATURAL", but as long as you and GOD know; that's all that matters. My intention to be around gossipers is to show God's glory so that others can see the change in me and know that they can also be changed. Well, as gossipers that's miserable and some people will be miserable for the rest of their life. But there should come a time in a person's life where you want to make a change and mature and see life in a different perspective and give people the benefit of the doubt and say "WOW"...that person has really changed, and the God is doing wonders in that individual's life. We as people come to a higher dimension in our life where you have to stop worrying about what people think and worry about what God thinks about you. Then you become so close to the master and he can use you as his willing vessel. Once you become in God's perfect will, you can understand the directions and purpose of the plan that God has for you from the foundation. And it sure is not to GOSSIP!!!

Our tongue is fire, and if you equip your tongue and minister to those who are going through the same struggles in life that I experienced, and be real with ourselves, and put self aside and let God work through us. God is a liberator; he has given us freedom so we don't have to gossip. Let's learn to love and be real with one another so we can become prosperous in life. When I became a soldier in the army of the Lord and dedicated to the service of God's assignment or church, we would say but don't get mixed up people with the word 'church' which again I tell you is just a building four walls. I am the church, the tabernacle, the chosen one!!! But the scripture still relates to not forsaking the assembly (fellowship) ourselves together as to how some are, but exhorting one another and so much the more as ye see the day approaching. I have been so confirmed to my word besides gossiping, the word becomes a lamp unto your feet and light unto your path. Without the word there is no direction, without direction there are no instructions and no instructions without a pastor who God has sent.

> *EPHESIANS 4:29 Let no corrupt communication proceed out of your mouth, but that which is good to the use of edifying, that it may minister grace unto the hearers.*

Most of all, if we learn to reject our own thoughts and fill our heads with positive thoughts there won't be any room for negative ones.

> *2 CORINTHIANS 9:6 But this I say, He which soweth sparingly shall reap also sparingly; and he which soweth bountifully shall reap also bountifully.*

> *PROVERBS 11:18 The wicked worketh a deceitful work: but to him that soweth righteousness shall be a sure reward.*

We have to learn to evaluate ourselves, and things, and move on. My entire life, I had gossipers who had lied about me, but as long as you know that you didn't perform in the action it never became a problem - especially if you know the truth. People wonder why folk don't basically indulge or trust others. Because as soon as you need to vent to somebody you believe in, that person is the first to go and lie and twist the story around.

I had received a promotion to a new hospital working after a long journey of accomplishing my goals and God finally put me where he wanted me to be. I had not been there 90 days; the first two weeks it was so many lies and stories told to my manager. Now, remember - this was the director of the company who actually called me in for the interview. When I walked in the door, I approached her with respect and honor but she got up and left out of the office. She never said anything else to me, but her knowing that God had a plan and what he has for me, no man can take it. She was already leaving the company in a month but did everything she could to fire me before she left, listening to the enemy (gossip) instead of getting to know me inside out. But GOD is a man that does things suddenly and he sent an angel in her position who to this day respects me and is willing to do what's right by her staff. God will send angels in the midst of your storm and will go with you throughout the storm, and you coming out victorious.

In the book of ROMANS, Paul reveals the sinful nature and lawlessness of mankind, stating how God poured his wrath on those who rejected his laws. Because they had turned away from God's instruction and guidance, he gave them over to their sinful natures. ROMANS 1:29-32; this is a real serious passage on the sin of gossip and who are under God's wrath. Widows were a specific group, and today they still are. They wait until they get old and miserable and want to look down on the youth and gossip about what they should or shouldn't do. We sometimes get older and become widows and forget how we used to get high, turn up, back it up, having all the fun and now want to have no life and sit around with nothing to do but gossip about others. Paul cautions widows against entertaining gossip. They were recognized as busybodies, saying any and everything that ought not to.

> *1 TIMOTHY 5:12-13 Having damnation, because they have cast off their first faith. And withal they learn to be idle, wandering about from house to house; and not only idle, but tattlers also and busybodies, speaking things which they ought not.*

That's ridiculous that Paul even describes it in the bible how the widows went from house to house looking for something to occupy their idleness.

Idle hands are nothing but the devil's workshop and God cautions against allowing that in our lives. A gossip betrays a confidence; so, avoid people who talk too much.

> *PROVERBS 20:10 Divers weights, and divers measures, both of them are alike abomination to the LORD.*

I have learned that when I open my mouth, it's positive vibes exhorting to the person I'm addressing my message to. If you want to listen or not, it's your choice. Yeah!!! Liz always talks, but I cannot help that I was blessed with a mouth to prophesize over people's lives and see transformation and manifestation in others' lives. As long as I was cursing people out and gossiping you guys loved me - but as soon as I put my hand on the plow to witness for God; here come the haters. God turns my mouth into MULTIPLE MIRACLES.

People, I acknowledge to you today that most of the time you can evaluate if the person is a gossiper because the gossiper is always accusing or discussing somebody else's issues. So, if you listen to that mess you would end up hating someone or falsely accusing a person you never got to know for something that's not true. I had to learn sometimes I might have brought up somebody's business - not to gossip but to use it as a testimony for someone else's struggle. If you find yourself speaking to someone that has no maturity and gossips all the time, you are making a bit of a mistake on sharing others' personal information or confidentiality. That's why I'm so glad that God has converted me to an area in my life where people trust me and I have secrets that people have trusted me with that no-one would ever find out. Tools you need to acknowledge when it comes to gossipers; be aware of what you say to others, stay off certain subjects, talk about good things to your friends, family, and associates. A gossiper only looks for acceptance, no one cares about you or the next person so basically, you are making a fool out of yourself. No-one's going to trust you; then you will lose friendship with friends that have been there for a lifetime. If you have a friend that you trust and gossip and tell your business to someone, just pray for them and eliminate what you discuss with the so-called friend. Play them with long handle spoon and handle it with sensitivity and caring. Also, cancel every assignment of the gossiper; the one that engages in gossip and those that gossip about each other as soon as they leave the person's presence.

I come against every lying tongue that rises up against the body of Christ and our families. I serve the enemy an eviction notice, to stop the whispering and talking down on one another, the tittle-tattle and the dirt that has been said against one another. I prophesize over anyone who is reading this book and anyone in the presence of this book that I cast down every tactless tongue, every argumentative tongue, every belittling tongue, and every complaining tongue, false accusation against others, cursing tongue, and any tongue that rises up against the knowledge of GOD. I decree and declare that our imagination, thoughts, ego, emotions come back into the obedience of Jesus Christ which is within us.

> *EPHESIANS 4:29 Let no corrupt communication proceed out of your mouth, but that which is good to the use of edifying, that it may minister grace unto the hearers.*

Now, if God is announcing that no corrupt talk comes out of your mouth how do we expect to receive the promises of God? We have to build one another up, so if we are communicating with someone that's listening let them hear a word of encouragement not to beat them down.

> *PROVERBS 6:16-19 These six things doth the LORD hate: yea, seven are an abomination unto him: A proud look, a lying tongue, and hands that shed innocent blood, An heart that deviseth wicked imaginations, feet that be swift in running to mischief, A false witness that speaketh lies, and he that soweth discord among brethren.*

I am just a messenger and a disciple.

LET'S WORK ON THAT TONGUE!!!

6 OVERCOMING GRIEF

In 2007 I lost a very special dear 'Woman of God'!!! My mother, my friend, my rock. Not only did I lose my mom, but I also lost three brothers out of nine boys. T.Bob (what they would call him), Chester who was better known as Hawk, and Tyrone – I also lost four favorite aunties to cancer, one was my mother's sister – Aunt Odessa out of Georgia, ATL and one of my favorite, favorite aunts Josephine (we called her sister) and the other two were my dad's two sisters Roaslee and Vestie. I also lost a favorite sister-in-law, Veronica who had been in our life since before I was born; for at least 40 years. My favorite uncles; Tea, Joe, June Bug, Spurge and my uncle Jerry and Pig; who were called 'big and little hutch' the mafia of the brood as well – so that leaves my mother's side of the family with just us who are the next generation to fulfill the dreams that she planted. All those deaths took place within a 10-year period besides Spurge and June Bug who had passed a long time ago; who was my mother's brother, one rich uncle from California who sowed the seed and that's why I'm reaping the harvest. It's so amazing how people look at you on the outside and never could imagine how you suffer in secret for years, bereaving over loved ones.

My uncle June Bug was a Marine, and the reason I moved to California

It was like every time God gives you the peace in the situation then "BAM"!!! Here it comes again, back to back. But I never cease to worship and trust God through the painful moments. Especially growing up around a huge family; mom from the ATL and dad from Vicksburg MI, most of those parents from the south had those huge families. Well, I guess picking cotton and corn and making five cents an hour, you know the economy was different; they had candles at night, no television and listening to the radios.

My mom and I were very close and one thing about me; I wanted to know everything so I would just sit with her and reminisce with her on how life truly was and the things she used to share with me about her times and how they actually lived. Just imagine if our generation didn't have the technology they have now - it would be higher suicide rates than it already is because people seem to not be able to cope without it. It's like they're God – children and teenagers waking up to games and everybody waking up to Facebook and Instagram before they can say 'Thank You, Jesus'. I believe if you really look at our ancestor's times and now it was a more secret and good life because everybody had large families, our fathers were dedicated and determined to go to work every day. It wasn't hustling because it was the faithfulness, and to have that many children in our household for my dad to be talking about taking a day off or hustling...these men worked because they knew they had families to feed every day and couldn't live off of hustling, because there were ups and downs. Well, I can recall when my mom was so pretty and young and she used to tell me the stories when she worked in the bars. WOW! Remember everybody wasn't always so holy and saved, but she was rooted in Christ from my great granny, Vollie Mary and her mother, Sallie B. So, I guess that's where I got my spunk from. LOL!!!

The family matriarch, Sallie B.

Well, my dad met my mom working in a bar and he said he would go in there every night and flirt knowing that he thought he was the finest brother on the block; which trust me I know he was because he is 82 and he's still got it going on. Yeah! My mom told me she made bank working in the bar and told me how her cousin used to hang out with her but I'm going to leave that alone...I don't want no problems. It's so amazing how we can look back over our lives and think about what our parents and ancestors have been through and then we experience the same motives and ethics through generations. Some can be blessings, and some can be curses.

As we grew up, I can recall staying on Wabash and Ash on the deep west side; I was the youngest where I attended Owen Elementary and my mom was a lunch aid, we came from the hood!!! I was born at Detroit Memorial Hospital in downtown Detroit, was always a Detroit legend so don't get it twisted because I transitioned to the rich suburban areas in my life. That's just to let the enemy know I can live and be anywhere my heart desires and where God wants me to be.

I really miss my mom and siblings who have died and gone on with the Lord. You know, grief is a multi-faceted response to loss, particularly to the loss of someone or something to which a bond was formed. Grief has an emotional response to loss, cognitive, social, spiritual, physical and philosophical dimensions. Bereavement is the state of loss, grief is the reaction if your loss and a variety of loss throughout your life such as dealing with employment, relationship, or health. There are stages of grief that I can present to those dealing with it; maybe as you read this book and the steps of the process are natural and healthy. Destruction and dangerous can become very unhealthy.

Everything in your life has a spiritual indication, God allows things to bring about in his divine purpose. Just imagine somebody so close to you is here today and gone tomorrow. Waking up from just burying a loved one and it's still fresh like one day or a week old and you still mourning and that individual no longer exists in the natural world... Yes, it's a hurting cycle, but know that Jesus wept and if he cried out to his father, then we can cry out to the father too and he will hear your cry. I want to recall a woman in the bible by the name of Naomi who was an Israelite woman. During a famine, she had gone with her family to live in the country of Moab. When her husband and two sons died, now can you relate to losing a husband and two sons? WOW!!! I know I'd be suicidal. But anyhow, she decided to return to her home town which was Bethlehem. She also had two daughters-in-law, Ruth and Orpah, and the story goes on, but back to the grief to lose a child and husband I'm quite sure can be very devastating. Just imagine; my brother T.Bob who admired me so much, who always came to my activities when I was in a dancing group and would be in competition at the carousel skating rink and traveling east and westside of town competing in dance contests; he was always there with me. One day out of the blue, he was hanging out on Visger Road (we don't know to this day if he was buying or selling narcotics) but a white man dragged my brother from Bassett and Visger all the way to Fort St and broke his femur bone and left him for dead. That's the strongest bone in your body which is the thigh bone if you're not familiar with the area. I mean; he dragged him two miles, he ended up in the DMC hospital had multiple surgeries and ended up dying from other causes and not only that he died on my son's birthday. As soon as we left the party at Chuck E. Cheese's we were walking in the door and the phone was ringing and me and my mom looked at one another and felt something's not right. On our way from the party it was raining cats and dogs, so that's normally an indication of something about to happen if you can relate. It was the DMC and all I can hear is my mom screaming. Man, oh Man! That hurt us so bad, especially from one of my brothers who had always protected me. Yes! It looked like a hopeless situation and I know God allowed certain things to happen and I'm not saying God does wrong things to people, but sometimes in life, some things are just allowed from the choices we make. God gives life and he takes life back, but he will keep your sanity and in your right state of mind through the storm of grieving. I wanted to throw in the towel plenty of days, and go back to my old ways, but the Holy Spirit would remind me to hold onto God's unchanging hand. We cannot operate in our flesh. What do we do when life has dealt you a bad hand? Naomi did it; she said, "I'm going back to the house of bread". I myself cannot go back, even though Orpah kissed Naomi and told her to go her way.

The death of my brother T.Bob hit us all hard

Now, if a person walks away and leaves; you don't try to force them to stay. Let them walk!!! Remember, your destiny is not tied up in that individual, your destiny is tied up in the will of God. Well, there are always going to be life and death issues and just like that the situation with Lazarus and his sister Mary and her dad called upon Jesus for help. God does not have to move on our time he moves on his timing. He allowed Lazarus to stay in the tomb for three days and then he said 'I'm going to show them who I really am and that I am the RESURRECTION"!!! He let him lay there for four days.

> JOHN 11:25 Jesus said to her "I am the resurrection and the life. He who believes in me, though he may die, he shall live, and whoever live and believes in me shall never die." EVS

When Jesus spoke about life and death, he spoke basically how someone dies and lives; he was talking about a kind of death physically and spiritually. Some people are live physically but dead spiritually and mentally because they have not been transformed by the renewal of their minds.

> ROMANS 12:2 And be not conformed to this world: but be ye transformed by the renewing of your mind, that ye may prove what is that good, and acceptable, and perfect, will of God.

Back to the stages that we can overcome and defeat in the grief process. It's something that you will never get over, but you CAN get through it. We will experience the first step of shock and denial; I went through this my people and it was crazy. I was not believing that this was really true or happening - it can last almost up to three months. Then you will experience intense concern which might last for approximately six months and that's where your lost and loved one keeps appearing in your consciousness and you just cannot stop thinking about it. It's not easy!!! You then face a trial of despair and depression which is sadness, anxiety, despair, feelings, guilt. I never experienced guilt because I always was there for my mom and I knew she was with God, and most people go through regrets of things that you might have not shared or talked about when that loved one or individual that was living; so people I know you might not be a gabber like me, but learn to share your thoughts and open up and communicate more with your friends and loved ones so you won't take guilt to your grave.

But, Oh! My! God! I truly experienced the other behaviors through every death and I'm quite sure we all have and will. So, I advise you to love your people and try to stop being so divided and so busy in life where you cannot spend time or pick up the phone and contact someone to say you love them or just hello. Now, this is the Recovery stage which is a new interest in functioning day by day, moment by moment, and we have to reorganize our daily walk and keep our mind stayed on Jesus because he said he will keep us in perfect peace. Even when you discover the pain and grief it doesn't hurt as bad if you most definitely be around motivating people who will trust God and encourage you to get through. You have to go through a coping stage as far as questioning your religious belief; the enemy will have you giving up on God and especially feeling like you are crazy. So, make sure you get support and connect with others that will pray and help you heal; draw your comfort from your faith. You have to have strong faith, even a therapist or a counselor if you don't have the faith, someone who can guide you through.

R.I.P my brother Hawk, always missed

I'm acknowledging in this chapter some loyal friends and families who experienced grief, and I want to leave this in memory of Zavier, my son's best friend who grew up together since they were kids – we love you Zay, and you will always be remembered. Kenna, a great friend of my brother Raymond who died of a sickness who would be at my mom's house every day; people thought he was our brother. One of my twin nephews' best friends; and he was one of the twin boys who my twin nephews hung out with every day. He got shot on Visger and my nephew saw his brains go on the ground. It goes on and on and on but my memories and prayers will continually go out to families who go through the phase of grief. I have to give all the glory, honor and praise to God because during the week of planning my mom's home-going it was so many demons that came up against me and people thought I would lose my mind. But me and my sister Patty, we let the Holy Spirit have his way and my aunt Edith, cousin Zenita, Reverend Felton and my one and only Pastor Smith; well, I would just say the Union Grace Missionary Baptist Church (which is my family church where my mom would take me for over nine years before I joined in 2005) they supported the family and me to the fullest. If it wasn't for them, I don't know; they were some praying warriors. One of the most devastating moments was during the week of planning the obituary when the whole entire family came to the funeral home to be noisy about what was coming out of insurance money when half of them didn't even speak to my mom. Then all the siblings came to my dad's house when he was bitter and didn't want anyone over, but I still step over his toes and let everyone come. Patty and I made sure everyone had their picture and a part in the service, so even through the bereavement there is going to always be a fight, but in the end, we still won the victory. My mother and my siblings are with the Lord.

PRAYER: MATTHEW 5:4...Blessed are those who mourn for they will be comforted. Lord God, you give and you taketh away. Lord, there is a beauty of grievances for a believer in Christ is that we don't grieve like the world does; we grieve as those who have hope. We will see our loved ones again and we will live with those in eternity. Family, I miss y'all but this is just a see ya later!

7 OVERCOMING DIVORCE THROUGH ADVERSITY

I know a good man; when I met him, it was all divine purpose and I followed all the instructions of what God had ordained for me to do to be a virtuous wife. Even with both of us going through uncertainties and vulnerabilities. Losing my mom, and he had been incarcerated for over 18 years. Me being rooted in the word and being taught the love of God from when I was a child, I was delivered from pride and I humbled myself to accept him for who he was because God can change anybody, and trust me he did. So, we as Christians and carrying these titles we have to not be so judgmental, but at the same time, the word says be equally yoke. I could truly say when I met this young man it was least expected and I was preparing for graduation and it had only been a year since we had buried my mom. Women and men, we have to learn how to hear God's voice.

> *JOHN 10:27 My sheep hear my voice, and I know them, and they follow me:*

God gives instructions and you gain knowledge and wisdom through the word of God. I am still growing every day and I don't regret nothing that God has allowed me to go through. I just thank God "In the name of Jesus" for the trials and tribulations because I learned from them. If I hadn't married and gone through the storm, I would've never made it this far and took a closer walk with GOD and become a lovely, loyal, purified, trustworthy woman for the husband that God has for me. So, we as the body of Christ have to continue to pray for discernment. So, when we do pray (which is the expression of mankind and communicating with God) we will make choices through God's will and not our own will. Being a powerful woman with an anointing to destroy the works of the enemy and being a prayer warrior, I can look back and laugh at the enemy because he thought through the manipulation, envious, jealousy and traps that the enemy had set up he lost the battle because God was with me all the time because his word states 'THAT HE WILL NEVER LEAVE OR FORSAKE ME'. The victory belongs to me. Victory has won.

In 2009, on October 16th (which was the day my youngest granddaughter was born) I remember it was a wonderful Friday morning; I woke up at 6am so excited about my wedding day. I'd not been able to sleep, wondering and meditating on how in just a few hours my whole life would change and I would be married. And not only my life changed, but my name also changed after 40 years! Staying up with my husband and reminiscing the night before and preparing our best gear out of the closet. We spent extra funds we know we needed to get my sexiest hairstyle for my wedding and being so excited to be married, not knowing that there was a giant to slay after we took this big step. As I drove, and the most beautiful smiles on both of our faces going to Toledo, MI to tie the knot. Now, we had been dating for a year and he had asked to marry me; which we were truly in love and we had communicated over most of our past and what the future would hold if we didn't allow the enemy to arrive. He already knew about me from a few family members who had been telling him to ask me out for a date. So, he already had the updates and heads up about 'she is nothing to play with', 'she's a good woman' and 'she loves the Lord', so he knew when he came into my life that he was going to be my husband. I had all the doors closed with my old boyfriends and yes, even though we eloped (everyone was so disappointed); but these same people I had known for over 30 years. Not knowing that it would affect others...maybe when I looked back, I could understand. Not that we don't have to be selfish and not tell people we are getting married, we are grown we are able to do what we please, but we have to be adults. Understand that life goes on and we as friends should always be happy for one another. Being the most honorable 'So got it together' wife that I could be my best, not perfect, but being perfection in what I had learned over the years of teaching and ministry classes and my mother teaching me how to be that virtuous wife.

> *PROVERBS 31:10 Who can find a virtuous woman? for her price is far above rubies.*
>
> *11 The heart of her husband doth safely trust in her, so that he shall have no need of spoil.*
>
> *12 She will do him good and not evil all the days of her life.*
>
> *13 She seeketh wool, and flax, and worketh willingly with her hands.*
>
> *14 She is like the merchants' ships; she bringeth her food from afar.*
>
> *15 She riseth also while it is yet night, and giveth meat to her household, and a portion to her maidens.*
>
> *16 She considereth a field, and buyeth it: with the fruit of her hands she planteth a vineyard.*
>
> *17 She girdeth her loins with strength, and strengtheneth her arms.*
>
> *18 She perceiveth that her merchandise is good: her candle goeth not out by night.*

You know we that were brought up in the word, and knowing God, we thought that the principles remained if you walk the walk, but if the companion is not walking the walk then the principles don't apply because some people have not experienced relationships or experienced principles of Christ. You can read all day and study until your eyeballs fall out, but if you have not been ordered by the steps of God it doesn't apply. My ex-spouse - he was always a kind man who was desperate for seeking

God's face, but he allowed pride and ego as a man to affect his nature and his household.

You know - I remember the ego seasons we went through but remember no-one's perfect and God can deliver anybody out of any situation if you allow God to dwell in your temple and work on you. Women and men; whoever is reading this testimony – it goes both ways, be careful what you pray for; be specific with God when asking for the desires of your heart. When you pray, you have to first trust and believe that the effectual prayers of the righteous availeth much. So, if your heart is not righteous, and you are not doing what God has ordained you to do, then you are praying for the wrong things and that's not good to pray and you not ready for marriage or for the promise that God has for you. Now, God is a prayer-answering God, but if he gives us our desires too soon and we cannot handle the position, we might end up right back in the same position. So, people; if you are not ready to build a family and a relationship that will lead to security and a soulmate like my mom and dad were married for 45 years and people that's married for 60 years - don't waste each other's time and space. Well, anyhow the day I eloped, wooh!!! Not telling no-one but my baby sister, and my daughter. I'm a grown woman and I don't have to give account to no-one but God. I had gone through a season where I didn't have a sister or mother in Christ that I could trust because us so-called 'holy thou art women' that I thought I could trust either hated me for being who I was or gossiped all the time or was envious of what I had.

My mother was deceased. I did have an aunt that I went to, Aunt Edith who always encouraged and supported what I did but always counseled me in the right direction. Which she told me; we don't believe in divorce and you can get married in my living room and not Toledo. Now see, that's God's voice right there; that we have to listen to and a person that's been in the vineyard a long time and a powerful person of God who knows how to be a good wife and a servant of God. But like we say – we are grown and we do what we want to do, so that's when we have to pay the consequences of life. Just remember, we have to be with a companion where you both are seeking the same desires. I never was the type of woman to spit venom on another individual. I always wanted what was best for others, but when you are sleeping with the enemy.... don't get me wrong, not my ex-husband, the enemy which are the spirits you are fighting daily. We fight not against flesh and blood, but principalities, rulers of the darkness, wicked people in high places, higher power. He had to discover his identity and not impress the world and learn to impress the master.

> EPHESIANS 5:33 Nevertheless let every one of you in particular so love his wife even as himself; and the wife see that she reverence her husband.

Now, don't get me wrong – in our first years of marriage we encountered some great times, one of my best friends and her husband took us and my daughter to their timeshare in Wisconsin for Christmas. Oh! What a great experience with our children, and being away so far and learning who we were and that life can be so beautiful once you experience the purpose of your excellence. We were in a hot tub at 30-below on Christmas and watching people skiing while we were connecting and just enjoying the love God has for us. Just because we experienced oppositions in marriages and relationships doesn't mean that there can't be beautiful times. You just have to keep your territory guarded and keep your armor on at all times and you can make it. How can two people walk together if two cannot agree?

Even though I accepted the engagement and the commitment of not fornicating any longer; respecting my Father's commandments, I suffered tremendously. WOMEN, MEN – DO NOT BE ANXIOUS FOR NOTHING!!! Even when a man looks good, ok, sounds good, we have to pray for, and hear the voice of the Lord and ask God to take the scales off our eyes to see in the spiritual realm and not the physical.

Now, women – when you meet these fine brothers and vice versa, men when you meet these fine women and you know the words says which is true, we have to pray and take everything to God in prayer. And, if we follow the principles, commandments, attributes of the word of God and fall in love with him then we would know the difference between just falling in love, lust, and infatuation. First of all – Love is God, kindness, generosity, self-control, purity etc. So, we have to know the difference between what true love is and not just falling for what makes us happy and going through the emotions in relationships. Don't get me wrong – we have all fallen short of the glory of God and we make foolish decisions and choices in our life, but after we have learned and experienced the same routine over and over and over again, why do we choose to go through cycles of generational curses and keep ourselves in bondage for year after year after year? Being in a relationship and believing for marriage and a prosperous life we have to not just be in a relationship because we got desperate, or we just want the sex because the man or the woman is so beautiful. Always remember; beauty is in the eye of the beholder and man looks at the outward and God looks at the inward. So, let's stop jumping into these relationships and enabling each other when we know we are not ready. We don't want to do these things so we can say that we have a man or a husband. Us women have to stop raising boys and us women have to stop giving up our goods to men that each one of us knows it's not true love and then we look up years ahead and we are hurt mentally, physically, financially, spiritually, because of our foolish choices.

    One of my biggest mistakes is being so generous, which is one of the fruits of the spirits that the enemy will use against you to get what he wants. But that's when he goes back to the word of God that says "greater is he that is in me than he that's in the world". So even if you make those foolish choices that are not in the will of God, just remember that we are greater than the worldly things and God will make you greater and he will give you greater and better relationships and the desires of your heart. People, we talk about in our generation that we're glad we didn't live in the times of slavery; but we ARE in slavery and bondage, due to the fact of the choices we make, which is what puts us in slavery and bondage. My ancestors conquered and survived slavery, so I know we can defeat the enemy because God has given me an anointing to destroy the yoke and bondage of generational curses and strongholds that the enemy had on me. I was this important person all my life to my friends, family, and relationships. So, I became a product of taking care of everyone and thinking I owed people and trying to please a nation and had to find out who the real pleaser was and his name is JESUS CHRIST. Not saying that I was this goddess, but sometimes people will put you on the pedestal like you are a GOD and you will get to thinking and believing that is why everybody is coming to me for help. Until I went through consecration, purification, shaping and molding through Christ, and then I understood someone else's struggle. Don't get me wrong – it's not that I didn't take care of me, but I didn't take care of me in the aspect of putting God first and then me and then everybody else, so in other words, I wasn't taking care of me. The word says "SEEK THEE FIRST THE KINGDOM OF GOD, AND HIS RIGHTEOUSNESS, AND ALL THINGS WILL BE ADDED'. That includes your husband, job, finances, etc. It's okay to help others, but don't be foolish and let folk use you. The only person that will use me is God as his willing vessel and for the building of the kingdom.

Whether you are choosing to divorce or have it thrust upon you, it is a time of adversity. It's how I viewed and handled adversity that determined how well I navigated the situation. One thing that I had to learn in life and in my marriage was that if you are not equally yoke or one in unity, it's not the perfect will of God. Every struggle and obstacle that we face in life, is considered a process of success protection and preparation. Another certainty that I can share, is to never get advice from single people if you are seeking advice for marriage. No-one can tell, teach or advise you nothing or direct you in the right direction if they have never been in that situation, or never walked in your shoes. We always have gossipers who are always on the outside looking in, but we have to trust in the mighty God so he can direct us and instruct us on the path that we need to take or exit in life. If we seek God's face daily, he will lead us into our purpose of what he has predestined from the foundation.

Well, I remember meeting my ex-husband on the fourth of July while I was very dedicated to the will of God. I had just graduated and accomplished my journey and completing my goals with an Associates of Applied Science degree in surgical technology. Would you believe how good God is, and how he sustained me during my years of education? And as soon as I was going to the next dimension and had an opportunity to go to Atlanta to travel as a surgical tech, me and my own decision-making stayed in Michigan and got married; so I had aborted one of my dreams to make a sacrifice for my ex-husband not knowing we wouldn't make it. One thing that I really thank the Lord for, is that I can stoop down to someone else's situation and make a sacrifice like God stopped down to the curve when the woman that committed adultery was thrown at his feet and they wanted her scorned but Jesus told her to go and sin no more. It's so amazing how we can sin and make mistakes and crazy decisions in life and God will sustain us. We have to lean not to our own understanding but acknowledge HIM and He will direct the path. Now, don't get me wrong –

my marriage was excellent in the beginning!!! Oh, I remember the first night which I'll remind my readers, it was the fourth of July. YEAH!!! Watching the fireworks with my family, daughter Niq, niece Cortrice and my baby sister Patty who was so amazed at how my ex-hubby held my hand walking in the park and picking flowers out of the Ecorse Community bushes. I hadn't been to the fireworks in over 10 years, but I decided to support the ones I love and enjoy the moment of first love again. Oh!!! How amazing it was, especially when it had been some time since a man had given me flowers. Well, what women don't want to receive beautiful roses? I had been in my secret closet with my relationship with God since I had joined my family church in 2005, which I was raised in a COGIC church, but was attending my uncle's Baptist church where I was called in that season. Where my ex-hubby was converted from a Muslim to a Christian through watching my faithfulness and daily walk. WOW!!! We never know what God has in store through the journey. We know as ambassadors and disciples as soon as we accept the mandate and the calling of Christ, here come our adversaries. Do not distract yourself from the joy of life by focusing on your shortcomings, or those of your ex-spouse. Remove any obstacles, emotional issues, gossiping, blameless thoughts you have of who did what wrong out of your head and replace them with positive thoughts that will teach you tolerance, for yourself and ex-spouse and your future. Through my marriage and relationships, we most of the time did things and made choices of our own will and not the will of God. And what's so deep about God, his thoughts are not our thoughts and his ways are not our ways. Greater than the Heaven above, his thoughts and ways are greater than ours.

The hardest and most painful season in the marriage was my ex-hubby not being employed and I was the breadwinner at the time and all the in-laws and so-called friends and haters used that against our marriage. They claimed they knew him, and jailed with him, which they never visited him in the 18 years he was incarcerated, so how was a person any support when you cannot support me when I'm down? Why would we allow the enemy to come in when you coming up? By him being such a great guy, he loved his family and friends but we have to watch families and the ones we love so much because those can become your worst enemies.

DO NOT BE CONFORMED OF THIS WORLD BUT BE YE TRANSFORMED BY THE RENEWING OF YOUR MIND!!!!

Trust me, as much as you might dislike your ex-spouse, they probably dislike you even more - we all go through bad times, obstacles and struggles, but that doesn't mean we as humans are not worthy of civility. I thank God that even though I went through jealousy, hatred, envy; I would never want to see anyone go through that situation. It was scary because I thought marriage was loving, kindness, joy, peace and happiness, but we allow people in our circle so get ready for the "RIDE OF DESTRUCTION". Even knowing that a mother-in-law can disguise and be so judgmental of you because of how you look, or your complexion, and not even getting to know a person internally. I might not like every woman my son had, but at least I got to know them, and as long as they treated him with love and didn't harm him, I love what is best for my son.

I just continued to pray daily and interceded for my husband and everything that existed around him that didn't want us together. The hardest delivering season I went through was praying for my enemies, but we have to draw the line at one point, we have to know that God is the manufacturer of marriage and he will see you through. But we as women, including me, have to be patient. The word says a wise woman knows how to build her house and I did, but I was not delivered from my stubborn issues and still a little pride. God says all things have to be done in decency, and in order, and in moderation. I was looking at the way of escape, besides continuing to pray for God to deliver my husband. Where I went wrong was when my husband begged me to come back home, and I refused to allow him back so he decided to drink and blame me for almost becoming an alcoholic and that's how the enemy stepped in. He ended up being weak and indulged with another woman, being intoxicated and "BAM" there's his little girl we had prayed for. You never know how GOD works; because this old woman wasn't trying to have any more babies after my daughter was 13. I was just still dealing with being stubborn and that woman who just wasn't taking no mess out of a man when no matter what relationship we get in, or marriage, it's always going to be oppositions and challenges of life. We just have to bear the cross, pray, trust GOD and obey.

My ex-hubby came to me after we separated in December of 2011 and he came to me as a man, and God had delivered him and exposed to him the enemies that tried to destroy what God had put together because what God has put together, no man can destroy. I just want you couples and people that are married to never give up on what God has put together. I let him come back, he went to the New Year's Eve service where he was delivered and wanted to restore the marriage but when he told me that he had committed adultery, God had made a way of escape and I just couldn't continue to be with my ex-husband.

EXODUS 20:14 Thou shalt not commit adultery.

I had not been delivered in that area of my life, but we have to understand that God forgave us, so I did forgive him. We left on good terms and no regrets. I just look at it as a life experience and to prepare us for greatness for our next relationship or marriage. I accepted my situation and stopped trying to change it. In a divorce situation, you have the power and total control over what path and what life your future will lead to. We don't have ownership over the enemy, and know that we have adultery, fornication and so on; we can accept that we have a problem we can never be that holy husband or wife. If a man or woman is not faithful to God, they are not going to be faithful to each other. No matter what we do in life if we don't break the cycle our children and children's children will have to face the same obstacles. You can be saved, and have an anointing on you of the perversion. If you aren't delivered from your bondage, you will have that same curse in your bloodline. I destroy every stronghold and bondage that the enemy has tried to set up. I cast down every trap, witchcraft, incantations, etc. that the enemy has tried to destroy over me, my family and anyone reading this testimony; we are delivered and set free from the bondage of the enemy. We can begin again!!!

I married a man whose identity had been stolen from the system and the culture of our lifestyles that we choose. Being rebellious and so anxious to experience the things of life, the enemy has tricked us and confused us and distracted us from our purpose to fulfill. I have learned on this journey that I should have let him experience his life, and live his life coming from being incarcerated for 18 years and let him heal from his past and his circumstances and letting him adapt to society after what he had been through. I had a great experience to learn that I cannot change people,

I can only change myself – and all things happen for a reason.

My marriage was so admiring and understanding in the beginning, like any relationship when you first meet a person; no matter what the past is, or what is down inside until we expose and open up the real package. That's when things really hit the fan and reality sets in. My ex-hubby was a very intelligent, trustworthy, loyal man. After our first experience of meeting and getting to know one another, it was very difficult for him coming out of the penitentiary as a Muslim and happening to meet a powerful woman of God. Walking a totally different walk; to this day I know it was strange and a very, very big change for me and him. Not only a change for him having his freedom back, but adapting to society and trying to get back all the things that he lost in life in 18 years of being incarcerated. But we make our own choices in life, and being kids and teenagers, we had to knock our head up against a few walls for thinking we know everything and being disobedient to our parents. The word says train up a child in the way they should go and they will never depart. So, thank GOD for our parents; they were parents who knew God and were rooted from the foundation. We still have to make decisions in our lives and the choices we choose to take. His family had a great impact in his life, his uncle a pastor and a great foundation for when he came home from being incarcerated.

PRAYER: Lord, help us to make wise choices when we date; and vulnerable with the uncertainties in life. Lord, even when the enemy comes to divide relationships, and divorce us, allow us to stand on your word and trust you more besides taking things in our own hands. Lord, what you put together no man can separate us from your love.

8 OVERCOMING PROCRASTINATION

Procrastination robs you of opportunities for service. It's a spirit of being slow or late about doing something that should be done. Why delay doing something until a later time or date when you can take care of it, RIGHT NOW? Because we have a 'right now' God so let's get it done right now! Why continue to practice carrying out less urgent tasks in preference to more urgent ones?

MATTHEW Chapter 26 relates to one of the most procrastinating stories in the new testament of an opportunity that was missed from laziness and could never be retrieved. The night Jesus went into the garden of Gethsemane on the night of his arrest and betrayal. Jesus took three disciples; James, Peter, and John knowing that he can count on those brothers (disciples). Now, if Jesus couldn't count on his disciples how can we count on each other in this day and time? Jesus went to pray three times and they fell asleep not knowing the significance of what was happening at that moment. But we never recognize being lazy or putting things off for another day would never replay the events of our life. Never let the enemy of doubt and procrastination keep you in despair. Never let anything stand in the way of your legitimate calling and keep being lazy and putting things off when you can take care of that matter right now.

God is a 'right now' GOD - QUIT PROCRASTINATING!!!

I remember a season in my life when I knew that I wasn't in the perfect will of God because I didn't know my purpose, but I knew what God had promised me. I knew that I was more than a conqueror for them who love Christ, Jesus. But I allowed that demon (spirit) procrastination tell me I don't need to register for school now, do it later, do it next year. I've been writing this book for 10 years. And that's why we cannot receive what God has for us because we contemplate, and get lazy, and are always putting what God has for us on hold. That old procrastinating spirit always tells you to finish it tomorrow. That's a bad influence and I advise you not to listen to it. We have to take control of that procrastinating spirit and stop putting off important matters we can accomplish today and not next week or tomorrow. We don't know that next week, or next year might be too late.

There was a time in my life when God had put loved ones and people in my heart knowing I should have taken a moment to call or pray for that individual, but I would say "I'll call them tomorrow," then tomorrow I'd say "I'll call them tomorrow". The same spirit of procrastination on and on and on. Then, when I finally decided to contact that individual, they were either in the hospital or dead. Sad, huh?! So, it was a hurting feeling, and I had to repent and go cry out to God because I took things in my own hands and not listening to the will of God. If I would have obeyed the will of God and not allowed the spirit of procrastination to affect me, people's lives that I was accountable for could have received a message from the Lord if I was obedient. Now, I withstand the wiles of the enemy of procrastinating. We need to get off our lazy rumps and walk into the purpose of what God has for us.

There's a cost when it comes to discipleship. We say we are followers of Christ and we are in His will. How can we be followers of Christ when of course we think of all the other reasons why we cannot respond to the call of our life? We have to take care of everything and everybody else before we decide to be obedient to the call of Christ. I had to learn (and it's not a good feeling) to have to go through so many struggles, trials, tribulations and obstacles before I decided to listen to the call of Christ and accept the fact that it's not about us. Don't get me wrong, there is an appointed time for every season but there were times where I missed my season for being a procrastinator. Before I can witness or sow seed in somebody else's spirit, God had to humble me and transform me and work on my patience. Most of all, I learned to listen. So, what are you worried about what Liz did in the past? Old things are passed away and all things become new and we become new creatures in Christ. We might not do everything right, but we don't do the things we use to do or continue to be naïve to the fact to make the same choices and mistakes. YES!!! It was painful for this woman, the old Liz who knew everything. For the woman who could manipulate every man for what she wanted and had the body of a brick house, and beautiful face and very talented. Of course, I had it going on so they agreed to take care of me because a strong woman has control of every situation if you know how to use it if you sisters understand where I'm going. I was raised from a family of God, but I didn't know him personally. I knew him from my mom introducing me to him and growing up in a culture of tradition - which don't get me wrong, it still paid off. I had to get to know God on my own and that's from the journey and the path and the choices and mistakes I made along the way that taught me that he is a keeper of my soul. That God is a bridge over troubled water, that God will heal the broken-hearted and the wounded. So, there is a difference in knowing God and knowing him as a personal savior for yourself!!!

Without God there is nothing. Even through my season of procrastinating I was so blind to the fact that I didn't even recognize that I was indulging in the event of procrastinating, because I was always a woman who would have or do what I wanted. But at this particular season that God had given me a spiritual eye to understand that I didn't have to procrastinate anymore; that I can just step out in faith and go for what I know and believe in myself and not try impressing no-one but my savior.

> *MARK:10:46 And they came to Jericho: and as he went out of Jericho with his disciples and a great number of people, blind Bartimaeus, the son of Timaeus, sat by the highway side begging.*

Have mercy on me, sometimes people we just have to hollow out and cry out to mighty God with a war cry to have mercy on us so that we can see in the spiritual realm. Then we can stop procrastinating and having scales on our eyes. I remember through my prayer life and falling prostrate on my face and being in the 'holies of holies'!!! Some people didn't understand that level with Christ and today some still don't but sometimes you just have to holler "ABBA FATHER"!!! And let God know that you can come before him naked and not caring what anyone says. I'm bowing to you, God, and trusting in you, because it's you who heals, it's you, God, who set the captives free. It's you, God, who brings us out of the darkness and into the marvelous light. Everybody can praise and worship, but praising God is when you can thank him for what you got. A true worshipper can praise God when your back is up against the wall, and you have lost your job or your only income. And you are at home lonely and wondering when the next miracle is coming and you can still worship and pray for your enemies and family and even the employer that fired you. God inherited the praises of his worshippers. And if just one of his disciples has a war cry...

Blind Bartimaeus had a loud war cry!!! Many haters, unbelievers, people rebuked him and told him to be quiet, but he insisted on shouting all the more.

"Son of David, have mercy on me!"

Now, check out my savior, JESUS STOPPED!!! Responded, and said:

"CALL HIM"!!!

Then the haters; the unbelievers, called to Blind Bartimaeus tell him to get up, cheer up, that Jesus was calling him. Jesus replied to Blind Bartimaeus.

"What is it that you want from me?"

Blind Bartimaeus said:

"RABBI! I WANT MY SIGHT! I want to see."

Sometimes we just have to be bold with Christ and just decree and declare what we want. And not telling or demanding God to do what we want, just being a believer and knowing what we want and having strong faith. And Jesus said:

"Go, your faith has healed you."

And immediately he received his sight and followed Jesus. That's a praise break right there.

HALLELUJAH!!!

So, people, we don't have to continue to stay blind. Ask God to give you a spiritual eye and start seeing your vision, your purpose, your way out!!!

NO MORE PROCRASTINATION!!!

Start crying out to God for deliverance and for the things he said that he would give your desired heart. Life is short. Life is precious, Life is good. Choose life and not procrastination because it's only going to stagnate you from walking into your purpose of what God had already predestined from the foundation.

> *JEREMIAH 29:11 "For I know the plans I have for you" declares the Lord "plans to prosper you and not to harm you, plans to give you hope and a future."*
> *ESV*

So, knowing that there is a plan for your future and not to harm you, procrastination will harm you and rob you of everything. Let's stop today and take the initiative to change from PROCRASTINATION to PURPOSE!!! Take off the mask and 'Walk the walk' and stop 'Talking the talk'. Just remember the times in our life where we know that we were supposed to get that task done and every time we put it off or rescheduled that situation. Believe me, you are going to have to complete it. If God says that he has begun a good work in you, trust me he is going to complete it and he will get the glory.

God's power to create life for us, to give us life, to bless our life and most of all, to give us everlasting life, is beyond our total comprehension of procrastinating.

PRAYER: Lord, rescue us from procrastinating, fear, and doubt. I pray you would quiet our stormy emotions and allow us to trust you in the most trying times. Lord, in a time such as this we cannot be like the sea wavering to and fro; so, we need your steadfast love to keep us knowing that with faith all things are possible through them that believe.

9 OVERCOMING LOW SELF-ESTEEM & IDENTITY ISSUES

In life, we conceive and become impregnated with our newborns and the families of what God has told us to subdue and take dominion over the earth. So, we are born knowing that we were predestined from the foundation and then we have the seeds of where our inheritance and legacy of who we are. Walking the journey of life from childhood to adulthood between that space we have choices, challenges, obstacle, opposition and even life's most difficult times; and we have some of the most basic explanation and the ability to comprehend and formulate practical ways to accept or change who you are at your core self. Self-identity, and the way you look at yourself and your relationship to the world. We have to learn to examine ourselves on an everyday basis especially when we get to a point of maturity in our lives, are knowledgeable and can understand life itself and know the creation of who we were made to be. Knowing our self-identity is understanding the personality, attributes, moral ethics, and also the knowledge of one's skill and abilities of what you can accomplish for life goals. Even during our stages of childhood and maturing into adulthood we also have to understand and determine what's our hobbies, our occupation and our purpose of what God has planned for us.

So, why - if we know that what is declared - do we have to have so much low self-esteem and always trying to tear each other down? And I'm just going to keep it real; when I was writing this chapter out of all the ones I wrote and meditated on, I might have had some issues in my life (as we all have), but I have never had low self-esteem about who I am. It hurt me so dearly to deal with friends, family and even men that I have dated in my life knowing that they didn't know their identity; so it affected my life and our relationships because of others not knowing who they were, and still to this day they don't know who they are. Men become inferior to others (and women as well) which is one generational curse that has to stop and be broken because families and friendships and even marriages are being broken because of self-identity issues. Now, if we know who we are, we don't have to not trust people in situations. I have had sisters-in-law who didn't even trust my brothers to be around me, and I would wonder back then what the hell is wrong with these demons? But when you don't trust yourself, and you don't know who you are, that's life and that affects other people's lives. My mother used to tell me these things and I'm so glad that I got saved and received by the Holy Spirit so now I can relate to the works and the word of God, and have a biblical understanding of why people think like they do.

> ROMANS 12:2 And be not conformed to this world: but be ye transformed by the renewing of your mind, that ye may prove what is that good, and acceptable, and perfect, will of God.

I know that there are people reading my testimony that may not have known or ever heard of God and were not taught the principles, attributes, and commandments of knowing God. And we know that we are still dealing with unbelievers, so I come as a believer and thanking God for my ancestors and my parents who knew God and introduced me to him. If you've read my other chapters, you know there's no way I could have made it without God's grace and a praying mother. I'm so excited that God chose me to write this book and to be an instrument to those even if you don't believe and want to receive the knowledge. I'm glad for my obedience; that out of millions of people that read this testimony, people's lives will be changed and transformed and I am a strong believer and I know that God's word does not come back void. It's not about me or the person reading it, it's about the assignment and taking my right place and seat and being obedient to the mandate that God has on my life.

Trust me, if it were up to me – I would not sit for four to five hours a day when it took me 10 years to complete this book. I was disobedient and I wanted to do things in my own way and God told me to complete this book because people wouldn't sit and listen to me, but they would pick up my book and read it. They would say let's see what she wrote, or can I write a book? Yeah, we all have a purpose and we can do whatever we want in life – that's when the self-identity steps in, let's stop talking about it and be about it. If God has begun a great work, he will complete it. I was wondering why so many doors were shut and that's because I wasn't listening and I was doing my own thing when I know I was pre-destined to be an author, when I know I was pre-destined to be an evangelist, when I know I was pre-destined to have my own business and my book become a movie.

We also have children that were raised and have low self-esteem about themselves and when children are dealing with low self-esteem, they have a difficult time dealing with problems, they become overly self-critical, they become passive, withdrawn from others and their peers and can become very depressed. Children that deal with low self-esteem can affect their thinking abilities, and they will become very frustrated and start speaking negatively constantly. Remove yourself from that atmosphere because it will drain your spirit and it is not healthy for your soul. So, just imagine how for a child, mentally can affect their way of living and growing up. It starts at home and if a parent or whatever adult is raising that child, we have to change our ways of talking, how we live, and how we do things around our children because when they start repeating from what they see and hear. Then we want to punish and curse at the children and beat the children and it's not the child, it's the parent who accepted certain things in the household that shouldn't never took place. That's why we parents - if it's one or two in the household - we have to cancel that seed before it even starts to grow. And get that seed at the root before it even flourishes and nourish them before it takes place. If I had listened to my mother back then, a lot of things my son and family wouldn't have had to experience. And don't get me wrong, the past is the past, but some people are still in the same predicament allowing the enemy and everybody else to control their children, their household, and think that everybody are your friends.

The same ones are in your face every day hating behind your back. I can say that, even though through my years of just not wanting to receive the truth. But now I can say I decided to follow Christ and I decided to listen, and I decided to make a change in my life so no matter what happened in the past I'm a new creature in Christ. Old things have passed away and all things become new.

I'm walking in new territory, I have new friends, I have a personal savior and I put him first, and he will give you the desires of your heart and he will make your life heaven and paradise right here on earth and you can have the most peaceful time of your life. When hell is breaking out all around you, God will keep you in the cleft of the rock and you will have so much joy and love and kindness and self-control and he will humble you; where you will be in the world, but not of the world. Dealing with self-identity as people, it can affect your child's stages of development. Then temporary problems can become permanent problems and we wonder why our children act so crazy and have problems in school and over the year look at the parents and the generational curses they are following. I wasn't the perfect parent, but walking with God and being brought up by great influence will make a great impact on your children. Also, if you raise a child up in the right admonition of Christ even if they stray; they are coming back to the purpose of what we have already planned for them. An example is how technology and the video games, the killings and the shooting and gang banging they are experiencing at the age of two; and you expect the children to grow up respecting the household? Now come on, be realistic. I had a friend that thought he knew everything and he used to buy his son all these games. The child was four years old and told his teacher that he was going to shoot up all the kids in his class and they called the police and he told the police at four years old that he was going to bomb up the schools and kill the police. He was kicked out of school at four years old – sickening.

Now, anybody in their right state of mind knows that's not funny and it's not appropriate. I'm not trying to tell people how to raise their children, but being out of purpose I had to deal with messy situations with my son, but I thank God he kept him. And it made me change my life so that I can be an example to my children and their friends and the world, so they can change and you'd best believe all my children's friends go to church and follow me. Even when they don't want to hear it, they know that serving God impacts something great in their lives. Even if they went to church, and then left the church and continue to be disobedient, it took time and a process. But I can look back and see how far they have come. I guarantee - and dare you - to try him and trust him; he will never leave or forsake you and his word will not come back void.

You don't have to be so holy and just give up everything at one time that you do in life; trust me, you read my chapters, it's a growing process and if you want to be converted God will be patient with you and keep you and sustain you and shape and mold you to the person he pre-destined you to be. People, I'm just an instrument and one thing I advise parents that are carrying their first child (and I know it's not easy) I carried a child nine months without a father or married or no help, God is your help. He will keep you, he will bring you through; so, as new parents, I give you this advice. INTERNALIZATION of self-esteem begins in early childhood. "IT STARTS IN THE WOMB!!!" Read to your children, sing to your children, because trust me they can sense and hear everything going on in the womb once they start developing. As children, and even adults, adversity and competition can ruin your life. We as people will challenge and experience these things in life, but the only way to get through it is to know your IDENTITY! Living a life with so much hatred towards me had become so devastating at one time in my life, but as times went on and I discovered my identity and understanding – it wasn't me it was the imps and the demonic spirits that had risen up against me and God had given me dominion and power to destroy the works of the enemy. And that's why I can love and learn to love my enemies because they didn't know any better. That's one of the most important things that others don't see or understand, especially when you have a personal relationship with the all-mighty. I did go through a time of my life when the enemy tried to turn me away from my loved ones because of so much jealousy, envy, intimidation and hatred and I wasn't converted to the point where I didn't understand what was going on. Now I can stand against the wiles of the enemy and fight against those spirits and love my people no matter what because of the love of God I have in my heart, and knowing my identity.

EPHESIANS 6:12 For we wrestle not against flesh and blood, but against principalities, against powers, against the rulers of the darkness of this world, against spiritual wickedness in high places.

To know that we are not fighting against our flesh and our own human beings and individuals, we can now come to our identity of knowing who we are and love one another as God loves us and learn to work on ourselves daily and walk into our destiny of life. God was present and people did not discern what he was carrying. We need to get our excitement back. I understand the mysteries of life and God gave you an understanding that life is worth living. The Holy Spirit will give you the way to make the right decision. I decree and declare that everything in your life will come back into divine alignment. As in 1 SAMUEL; I know who I am - we need to reconnect ourselves to God and get a complete understanding. We have to converse with God to know how to live in his strategy.

Life is not about biology, statistics, graphics... "God is the finisher and the author of our faith" that's why God picks certain people to perform his mystery. We get it twisted dividing ourselves into categories of life. One portion of people say they're upper class, the others say they're middle class and then the lower class... I come to tell you I'm not in no class with God, we are our own individuals, and that's where we get confused with our identity. Man-made and tradition and religion have distorted our nations and continent because we really don't know who we are. He created us in his image and likeness and he is everywhere, so that means we can be anything or anybody we desire to become. He will hold you together when you are falling apart, but we have to know our purpose and our identity first, so that God can work on us to be that great Doctor, Lawyer, Surgeon, Author or President and whatever you are pre-destined to be; and that's knowing your purpose and identity. God announces our comings, our goings. He knew us before we knew ourselves, and he knows every hair strand on your head, he knows all the 206 bones in your body, the 650 muscles, and the four chambers of your heart, and the external and internal of your body and all the 11 systems that function. So, you tell me how we can compete and let others discover who we are when all we have to do is go to the master and believe and take everything to God in prayer and he will answer? That's one of the reasons why we cannot get anywhere in life because we go to the wrong people who you may think have got your back and the answer to the solution, and that's the same enemy who is praying and competing against you and want to see you fall. So, I've come to tell you that if you trust God with your WHOLE heart, soul, and mind he will show you your real IDENTITY! One great thing about my SAVIOR – he accepted us before we accepted him. We only have to acknowledge his goodness, and greatness, and kindness; and follow him and let him direct and guide us all into truth and we will know who we are, and whose we are.

PRAYER: LORD God, when we are overwhelmed in life with low self-esteem and identity insecurities, remind us that we can go to the rock and lean on you when there is no-one to go to, Father, Lord remind us our battle is not with weapons, but it feels like it at times. Lord, I have fought this battle to love myself and to forgive those who have hurt us. Lord continue to remind us this battle is not ours; so teach us to stand and be still, because our identity is in you and you have the victory.

10 I CONQUERED IT ALL THROUGH CHRIST

Through this journey of life, being an overcomer and God destroying the yoke that kept me in bondage and captivity for so many years; it has been not only bearable, but it has been a great life experience. I always told my children and people after I learned the reality of life, that without going through the fire and facing life experiences - how would we ever know our weaknesses and know how to react through our most uncertainties of life? Being in the situation I am in now in Los Angeles, for five years taking a faith walk with $75 and a suitcase; my daughter who didn't want to come, but stood by her mom and my son who always said 'Mom you raised us, it's time for you to live'; and everyone knowing I was so overprotective of my babies and family. And I still am today; I will go to war today.

When I heard the voice of the Lord and he spoke to me to leave my kindred like he told Abraham and go to this far land after I asked and prayed to God. When I turned 50, I was done with Michigan and he told me as well that my mission was up and it's time for a new journey. It was between Atlanta and California; so that was a hard decision to make because that's where my mom was born in Georgia. But I had been there over 12 times every year down the roads traveling on buses for 16 hours with her; my children and my nieces. So, I prayed to the master again and again and again. Sometimes we think we are hearing from God, but do we really know him on a personal level?

MATTHEW 6:33 But seek ye first the kingdom of God, and his righteousness; and all these things shall be added unto you.

We know the scripture, and we talk about it and quote it, but are we meditating day and night; are we prostate on our face; are we praying like David did three times a day?

It's not easy being successful or even listening to the voice of the Lord. Because the first thing people would say is "How do we know it's God and not Satan?" Okay, since you asked!!! Studying the doctrine; personal bible study and praying without ceasing. Yes! It's millions of bibles written, but he said his sheep shall know his voice and follow him. When you follow Christ, you see signs and wonders; you see miracles like healing; deliverance and people being set free. Satan is not trying to set anybody free from bondage. Satan is trying to set you back. And I have come to reality to recognize that I have gotten confused about the word of God, but when he sent me to Cali in the cleft of the work and preserved me for only him until his purpose is being fulfilled, I learned to know His voice. Man cannot put you in million-dollar houses and sustain you with no job but remember it goes back to the word of God saying he will give you houses you didn't build and vineyards that you didn't lay and will definitely make your enemies at peace with you and your footstool.

When God gives you the vision, he will equip it with exactly what you need; THAT'S WHY BELIEVING IS ESSENTIAL.

When you are pre-destined and chosen, God takes time with you to make you into a jewel; we were created to be Queens and Kings, not called out of our names and we all have a gift and talents.

In the Gospel of MATTHEW 25:14-30…we find Jesus' Parable of the Talents…. He gave five talents to one servant, two to another, and one to the third; to each according to his ability. The master then left on his journey. So, when he gave me a few talents as a Surgical Tech, Evangelist, Missionary, Prophet, I took the step of faith and went on my journey and obeyed the call of Christ. So why do we get jealous, envious and intimidated by each other when he is not a respecter God? There's enough work in the kingdom for everyone, but the harvest is plentiful and the laborers are few.

So, I come to Prophecy; that everyone who reads this book takes a moment and believes that you are more than a conqueror who loves Christ Jesus; my mom used to say no-one said the road would be easy, but nothing's too hard for God.

People that walk in their blessings aren't envious or intimidated by others, but envy and jealousy come from the other entities that have not discovered their purpose. So, without discovering your purpose you will never walk into your destiny or dreams. God has a PURPOSE and PLAN for everyone. Step into your next dimension and take back everything that the devil had stolen. I renounce to Satan that he is defeated, and God conquered death two thousand years ago, and he has the keys to hell and heaven.

Don't give up on hope, because if you lose hope, you lose out on life and that's Satan's plan. How many times have you been stung and how many times you going to allow people to sting you?

We have been given AUTHORITY, DOMINION, AND POWER to arise above all storms; stop asking God to do everything and get up and do something (FAITH IS DEAD WITHOUT WORKS). All you need is the size of a mustard seed and mountains have to get out of your way.

Don't give your energy to your history; give your energy to your destiny.

When a man's ways please the Lord, he will make your enemies at peace with you and you can sit down and rest your foot on his footstool. People are going to do you wrong, and that's a part of your growth and maturing in Christ, but continue to trust God even when you cannot trace him and pray for those that know not what they do.

The most peace I ever had was forgiving my enemies and praying for them, but baby I had to question God on this one. Lord, how can I love people that hate and envy me? Okaaaay: again, keep the word in your heart so you might not sin against him.

JOHN 15:18 If the world hate you, ye know that it hated me before it hated you.

I had to learn on this journey to stop complaining about what we don't have, and what people don't do for us. Start thanking God for what you do have, and work with what you've got so that he can surround you with the right divine connection to get you to the next dimension. You might not see the external work, but as he works on you, and you allow yourself to be used as a vessel and move self out the way, the internal will start changing.

When you go forth, stop looking back to what's beneath you and press toward that which God is calling in front of you. He's always working on our behalf. We all have our own appointed time; it just hasn't manifested yet. See, we all want to be on the frontline, but God has not appointed us. So, watch what you are praying for, because only faithful, dedicated, and equipped soldiers are placed in the frontline and the battlefield is real. I never was a pulpit girl or a platform person. I came from the hood and I love my missionary work in the streets with the homeless and whoremongers, crackheads, etc. God cannot appoint you if he don't anoint you, and most of the time he takes you right back to the territory to save the same ones that you use to deal with; now that was the most devastating experience when he always take me back to Michigan after he removed you from your kindred, but back to Abraham.

Our love for people should be sacrificial because God loves us and he made a sacrifice and gave his son Jesus to save us from our sins.

> *JOHN 3:16 For God so loved the world, that he gave his only begotten Son, that whosoever believeth in him should not perish, but have everlasting life.*

I had to learn going through booth camp and seminary not to be so judgmental and quit beating people down, but it's good when you can admit your faults and then you can become a better servant so you can be used in the kingdom.

I love the story (one of my favorites) when God sent Moses back to Egypt to demand the release of the Israelites from slavery. After the ten plagues, Moses led the exodus of the Israelites out of Egypt and across the Red Sea after which they based themselves at Mount Sinai, where Moses received the ten commandments.

When we are being led and instructed on an assignment from God, first we have to have a listening ear and convert over into the kingdom and have a Christ-like mind. God told the Israelites to go on a journey for 11 days and they ended up in the wilderness for over 400 years. I have been there, stuck not only in my physicality but also mentally, spiritually, emotionally. I most definitely always had money and was always financially blessed, but there was always a hole in my pocket from being in bondage and spending it in the idolatry places; having millions and always broke.

People, God sometimes takes us through things that are not for us; it's to bring maybe your family, son, daughter or someone else from BONDAGE to FREEDOM and He gets the glory. It's not easy being a disciple and ambassador on a mission, not knowing what's going to happen. Talking about for God I live and for God, I die, and people hating you for being a servant. But I come to let the world know that if God is for you, then who can be against you and His word does not come back void.

Look at what they did to Christ - he had 12 disciples and Peter remembered the word JESUS has spoken just as clear; before the rooster crows you will deny me three times…I have that experience knowing, with the gift of discernment. I knew the friends and jealous ones that will deny me and betray me before it happened because I hung out with them for so many years and I studied friends and knew them better than they knew themselves The Gospel of LUKE 22:59-62 in the last denial… Peter replied:

"MAN, I DON'T KNOW WHAT YOU ARE TALKING ABOUT"!!!

Isn't it funny how the same people you thought were your ride or die; those who broke bread with you, lived with you, you clothed, took in and housed, gave the shirt off your back, but when you went through the storm they turned their back and said what are you talking about? LOL! WOW!

But I'm like Jesus; I still got LOVE for you. Because your highest elevation and success comes through haters and betrayal. And, of course, we have… JUDAS!!! Which we have a lot of those in our lives, I'm quite sure you can relate to that. Even though Judas was one of the closest ones that walked with JESUS during most of his ministry, but betrayed the Lord to the Jewish authorities. Watch who you walk with every day and who knows your every mood might just be friends of the 'AUTHORITIES'.

> *MARK 14:44 And he that betrayed him had given them a token, saying, Whomsoever I shall kiss, that same is he; take him and lead him away safely.*

The person JUDAS kissed was the one who was supposed to be taken away. Now, me myself; if I'm not mistaken, I thought a kiss was supposed to be like a sister or brotherly LOVE, honor. But most people that have kissed on me and on you as well, was a kiss of betrayal. Some kisses might be a kiss to get you in a position of bondage for the rest of your life, we get so comfortable with the romance and a man whispering in our ear because it feels good, but I break free from the spirit of lust and living in the flesh. Love is action and not betrayal!!! We have to watch who is kissing on us because we might just be sleeping with the enemy; so how you kiss me and betray me at the same time. THE DEVIL IS A LIAR. But sometimes it's a blessing to have a JUDAS nearby and your enemies near, because it brings the best out of you it lets you know that you are a person that's for greatness. Evidently, if you take out that much time to study me, I'm someone very special and you are afraid of me making it to the top. But I come to tell you again, being betrayed I had to die in the flesh and bring it under subjection; I felt like I was buried. But my God, my savior, my ROCK who they thought would not get up, ROSE FROM THE DEAD!!! Was RESURRECTED with ALL POWER and I've been RESURRECTED; my son and daughter, grandchildren, family and loved ones have been RESURRECTED. So, I took AUTHORITY, DOMINION, and POWER over captivity and bondage and wrote this book. Open that business, fight for your marriage and salvation, over your family.

God chooses people with a good sincere HEART; quit allowing your head to control you and let your heart be renewed through Christ Jesus. It might hurt, but we have to let some people go so that other great people with a DIVINE CONNECTION can enter into your new life of DESTINY and PURPOSE. So that you can exchange the PROPHECY over your life. Our PROPHECY and destiny can be delayed because of our cold hearts. Purpose can exist in a prison, 'desert', addictions; and when you know your purpose it keeps you alive. I made it on purpose. I could've died; but hatred, rejection and injustice couldn't kill me. I wanted to quit, but God kept me alive for a PURPOSE.

He will keep you in perfect peace if your mind is stead on him. So, are you going to allow your pride or ego to make your decision, or are you going to allow the mission to bring you into your position?

God always saves the best for last.

PRAYER!!!

You can accept Christ right now in your living room, workplace, bathroom, kitchen, club; grocery store; He is everywhere and He is waiting on you.

The steps to salvation:

ACKNOWLEDGE...you are a sinner.

> *ROMANS 3:23 For all have sinned, and come short of the glory of God;*

REPENT...realize the awfulness of sin and be sorry.

> *ACTS 3:19 Repent ye therefore, and be converted, that your sins may be blotted out, when the times of refreshing shall come from the presence of the Lord;*

CONFESS...Before God for Salvation.

> *ROMANS 10:9 That if thou shalt confess with thy mouth the Lord Jesus, and shalt believe in thine heart that God hath raised him from the dead, thou shalt be saved.*

FORSAKE...Sin, turn from, quit committing.

> *ISAIAH 55:7 Let the wicked forsake his way, and the unrighteous man his thoughts: and let him return unto the LORD, and he will have mercy upon him; and to our God, for he will abundantly pardon.*

BELIEVE...In the finished work of God on the cross.

> *JOHN 3:16 For God so loved the world, that he gave his only begotten Son, that whosoever believeth in him should not perish, but have everlasting life.*

RECEIVE...Him into your heart by faith.

> *JOHN 1:12 But as many as received him, to them gave he power to become the sons of God, even to them that believe on his name:*

From BONDAGE to FREEDOM

ABOUT THE AUTHOR

Mary Barber is an author, evangelist, entrepreneur and radio host. She hails from a large family in Detroit. Her upbringing challenged and strengthened her through both intense low points and amazing highs that shaped her into the passionate and determined woman she is today. With her children grown, she fulfilled a life-long calling to move to California and minister under Bishop Charles E. Blake. Mary loves living in California and knows that her faith walk has guided her to her home. She gained her Associate of Applied Science in Surgical Technology in Michigan and has worked extensively as a traveling nurse. Mary is passionate about encouraging, motivating and coaching others to achieve their dreams and overcome their circumstances - she also completed her Missionary Evangelist License and is getting ordained in 2020. She credits her father, Leroy with setting the example as an engaged and loving man who raised her with integrity and stood passionately by her (now-deceased) mother's side for 50 years.
When she isn't winning souls for Christ, Mary loves to travel, spend time with family, eat good food, write, exercise, meditate, go to the beach, bowl and watch movies to relax and unwind. Her dream is to open a transitional home for the disabled and mentally ill, and to build her own Mission Ministry in foreign countries to help those in need.
Mary has 2 grown children and 5 grandchildren. This is Mary's first book.

Look for Mary's next book (Coming Spring 2020)

$75 and Faith
The Transition

Made in the USA
Monee, IL
11 July 2020